THOSE ECCENTRIC YANKEES

THOSE ECCENTRIC YANKEES

EDITED BY **JOHN LOVELL**

INTRODUCTION BY
ROBERT TAYLOR
FORMER BOOK EDITOR OF THE BOSTON GLOBE

YANKEE® BOOKS
Camden, Maine

Every effort has been made to trace ownership of all copyrighted material and receive permission to reprint the articles. In the event of any question arising about the use of any material, the publisher, while expressing regret for any inadvertent error, will be happy to make the necessary correction in future printings. All articles are from Yankee Magazine *and are reprinted with permission.*

Cover design by C. MICHAEL LEWIS, Portland, Maine
Text design by AMY FISCHER, Camden, Maine
Typeset by TYPEWORKS, Belfast, Maine
Printed and bound by BOOKCRAFTERS, Chelsea, Michigan

Library of Congress Cataloging-in-Publication Data

Those eccentric yankees / edited by John Lovell.
p.   cm.
Includes index.
ISBN 0-89909-205-5
1. Eccentrics and eccentricities — Northeastern States — Biography.
I. Lovell, John, 1907–
CT9990.T58   1991
920.074 — dc20
[B]   91-10809
                                                              CIP

10   9   8   7   6   5   4   3   2   1

TO ALL **ECCENTRICS** EVERYWHERE

Contents

3

Performers and Prodigies

4

RISK TAKERS

Introduction

When I was eight years old, schoolboys dodging a haircut were warned by their mothers: "You'd better see the barber; you're beginning to look like Joe Knowles." Joe, the Naked Thoreau, had plunged unclad into the Maine woods and emerged two months later wearing a bearskin and flexing his biceps. His tangled hair anticipated the sixties by a half-century. Although his exploits had occurred in 1913, kids a generation afterward still considered him a folk hero.

Behind every eccentric like Joe, as Herbert Adams reveals in his delectable "Saga of Nature Man," lurks a public relations wizard. Unless the private affectation becomes a public attraction, the eccentric, however colorful, is destined to embellish the lively yet anonymous annals of local lore. Every New England town no doubt has a "character" on the order of fiddler and snowshoe designer "Mellie" Dunham, Norway, Maine's, answer to the Grand Old Op'ry, but not every old-time fiddler plays for shindigs by Henry Ford and finds the Stock Exchange on Wall Street closed a few minutes early to honor his visit.

In Joe Knowles's case, the wizard was Paul V. Waitt, who doubled the Boston *Post*'s circulation in two months with his vivid accounts narrated from Joe's point of view. (The New Adam, after all, should have been too busy surviving, though ostensibly he relayed his adventures to the *Post*'s editors via birch-bark messages tucked in the roots of a fractured spruce.) When I encountered Waitt some 40 years later, toward the end of his journalistic career, he still practiced his art and sullen craft. Soap Box Derby Editor for The Boston *Traveler,* he promoted a downhill race for boys. The contestants drove home-made vehicles cobbled from old cartons and bales of twine, although some of the sleeker cars appeared to have been designed by professionals not unacquainted with the principles of a wind tunnel. An elfin, somber man, Waitt on the face of it seemed the unlikely author of the epic feats portrayed in *Alone in the Wilderness: by Joseph Knowles,* but eccentricity sometimes characterizes the celebrator of eccentricity, too. Consider the supreme example of the father of literary biography, James Boswell.

During the 19th century Waitt's role was assumed by P.T. Barnum. General Tom Thumb, the wild animal collector "Grizzly" Adams (a forerunner of Joe Knowles), and Sylvia Hardy, the Lewiston, Maine, "giantess," were Barnum products, while the hirsute seven Sutherland sisters and Vermont's mathematical prodigy Zerah Colburn also pursued the will o' the wisp of show business fame. By what standard did Barnum judge them? As an eccentric he didn't have to look further than himself.

The quirks and airs of General Tom Thumb sprang from the attitudes of others toward him; his true eccentricity was in the eye of the beholder. So is the present-day behavior of Walter "Killer" Kowalski, the wrestler. He's eccentric owing to the contrast between his public personage as a ruthless monster, the Bigfoot of the ring, and his private self, mystical, nonviolent and as inclined to inhale fragrant blossoms as Ferdinand the Bull.

The canal networks that astronomer Percival Lowell assumed he saw on Mars are another instance — once seen by Lowell, these were also perceived by the leading astronomers of his day. Out of Lowell's absorption with Mars, though, emerged his interest in Neptune and the eventual discovery of the planet Pluto. Scientists only seem "mad" to us when their hypotheses go awry; suddenly their concentration upon a problem looks lopsided, and their authority erodes. Dallas Boushey's fascination with the subject of human anatomy seems eccentric as long as he's a $15 a week janitor in the animal research lab of the University of Vermont College of Medicine; but when he's designated a full professor for learning more anatomy than either the students or the faculty possess, his offbeat hobby takes on a different aspect.

Eccentricity, then, is subjective. But in its more familiar manifestations, we imagine the eccentric to be obsessed and single-minded — and we may be wrong. Sculptor Gutzon Borglum, a Czech Connecticut Yankee, not only carved Mount Rushmore, a feat requiring sustained larger-than-life concentration, but started a boxing club and helped draft the constitution for the Republic of Czechoslovakia.

Observe "The Original Human Fly," George Gibson Polley of Marblehead, Massachusetts. Was it obsession that drove him to emulate Harold Lloyd's thrill comedies and climb the highest building in the United States? Not at all. He did it "because it's there," the mountaineer might respond, but Polley's conquest of more than two thousand lofty urban structures was both philosophically daring and good for business. Richard O'Donnell's story follows a career that one-upped the assaults on Mount Everest, since in effect Polley was saying, "Granted, the natural obstacles on the planet have been subdued, but the challenges of architecture are forever." When it seemed that everything had been done that could be done in the Human Fly line, Polley proved infinitely resourceful. He was a practical fellow, a go-getter, the topmost New England huckster of the Essex motor car, and his breathtaking climbs were prelude to a sales pitch. Barnum himself would have approved.

As opposed to this, the grand tradition of mild lunacy implied by the word eccentric — like the chicken mania of Miss Nancy Luce of Martha's Vineyard — is amply represented. The apocalyptic preacher William Miller heard spectral voices and computed numerical prophecies based on Biblical sources. M. Robert Beasley's "The Man Who Drove A Million People Crazy" relates what happened when Miller's prophecies were taken literally by crowds across America on the night of October 22, 1844. One of the most tremulous gatherings that night consisted of a cluster of Millerites in white robes on the ramparts of a granite building in Boston — the Howard Athenaeum, soon to gain fame as the Old Howard Theater, a bastion of the bygone theatrical art of burlesque. There's a certain appropriateness in its origins as a Millerite temple.

Another eccentric on this order was Uncle Joe Holden of Otisfield, Maine, whose credo about the flatness of the earth derived from premises that would not have been outlandish in the Middle Ages. Thinking for himself — in this instance, not the most reliable of procedures — Uncle Joe attracted sold-out audiences to his lectures. Mrs. Frances B. Hiller's eccentricity lay in her belief that Kaufman and Hart were wrong when they said You Can't Take It With You; but in her attitude toward death she was not unlike the pharoahs of ancient Egypt. Hetty Green, the Witch of Wall Street, comes under editor John Lovell's heading of "Schemers" by way of contrast to Mrs. Hiller's "Dreamers." The getting and storing of money preoccupied Hetty whereas Hiller wanted her wealth to buy immortality.

Sometimes an eccentric qualifies as a result of an occupation or profession. David Park of Williams College never wore a watch, and Dr. J.T. Fraser liked to edit the interviewer's tape when interviewed via tape recorder, and R. Glenn Hall of the Naval Observatory adds a "leap second" to the end of every year, but surely these are trifles. Their mutual study is that most eccentric and fascinating of elements, Time. Ruth Stout's theories on organic gardening, which once seemed radical, no longer look eccentric in the late 20th century: James M. Whitney, the New Hampshire cowbell virtuoso; Larry Webster, from Rhode Island, who searches for downed and missing aircraft; and Hartford's pictorial historian, Tony DeBonee, are eccentric mainly by virtue of the peculiar flair they bring to their unusual pursuits.

Documenting communities and the people who live in them is not unconventional and has produced grants for many a photographer. Tony DeBonee, however, differs from the pros since he takes snapshots in order to record his memories. He's "the common man's amateur photographer," and, however compulsive, he captures a special angle of interpretation; he has been able to take pictures many outsiders wouldn't see right away or might consider beneath attention. The social values of eccentricity were discovered by New Englanders long ago. Other parts of the country might not perceive the usefulness of a 50-year-old man's talent for catching a grape tossed from the summit of a 528-foot building. Here it signifies the differences between us, the idiosyncracies we share; here Killer Kowalski and Percival Lowell meet equally matched.

Robert Taylor
January, 1991

THOSE ECCENTRIC YANKEES

1

MAD SCIENTISTS

Those Martian Canals

TOWARD THE END of the last century an energetic watcher of the skies initiated one of the hottest wrangles ever to embroil the scientific community by stating flatly that Mars was inhabited by creatures of superior intelligence and that the proof was there for all who were not too blind or pigheaded to see it. The outspoken astronomer — who was destined to achieve permanent fame for a quite different discovery — was a wealthy and peppery Bostonian named Percival Lowell.

The oldest of five children, Lowell was born on March 13, 1855. Apparently the family heritage included not only wealth and social position but also an unusual facility with language. His sister was Amy Lowell, the poet; his brother Lawrence became a noted scholar and president of Harvard; and Percival composed poems in Latin and spoke French fluently by the time he was 11 years old.

In 1876 Percival Lowell graduated from Harvard with honors in mathematics and took a year off to roam Europe and the Near East before returning to Boston and employment in the office of his grandfather. The new apprentice did not start on the bottom rung. In fact, in no time at all he was managing trust funds and acting as treasurer of a cotton mill. In a few years Lowell had accumulated a sizable fortune and decided to take a few months off. In the spring of 1883 he set sail for Japan.

Lowell was born restless. To him a vacation meant increased activity. Fascinated by Japanese culture, he rented a house in Tokyo, staffed it with servants, and went about learning the language with extraordinary swiftness. In August, at the request of the U.S. State Department, Lowell agreed to shepherd a Korean trade mission to Washington, afterward visiting Seoul as a guest of the Korean government. Lowell finally tore himself away to return to Boston and write a book: *Choson — The Land of Morning Calm.*

During the next 10 years Lowell spent a good deal of time in the Orient and wrote three more books: *The Soul of the Far East, Noto,* and *Occult Japan.* The three books sold well, for Lowell had a sharp eye for beauty — both architectural and feminine — and his prose was lively and colorful. His sense of humor ran to puns, and his writings were liberally (some critics charged excessively) sprinkled with them.

In 1893 Lowell suddenly shifted his attention from the Orient to wider horizons — or, more accurately, no horizons at all. For years he had made a hobby of astronomy and on his last trip to Japan had burdened himself with a six-inch-diameter telescope. Upon his return he resolved to build an observatory.

This seemingly impulsive decision had its genesis in 1877 when Giovanni Schiaparelli reported a number of long, narrow, perfectly straight lines on the surface of Mars. He referred to them as *canali,* meaning channels. He noted them again in 1879. In 1882 Lowell's nimble intelligence had grasped the implications of this discovery, and upon learning of Schiaparelli's impending retirement, he determined to embark on his own exploration of Mars. Lowell's interests included such varied activities as botany, hiking, polo, and reading everything he could get his hands on, but astronomy now became his ruling passion and was to remain so for the rest of his life.

Lowell went about selecting a site for his observatory in typically logical fashion. He was one of the first to fully appreciate that the main obstacle to accurate celestial observation is our own constantly swirling atmosphere, which causes the image in the eyepiece to shimmer. Stronger telescopes simply make a bad matter worse. The solution is to locate the observatory on some high, dry spot away from cities with their smoke and pollution. After considering locations in Mexico and the Andes, Lowell chose a hill near Flagstaff, Arizona. Money can work wonders; in less than a year the observatory was completed and three bungalows were erected for Lowell and his two assistants. From then on Lowell divided his time between Flagstaff and Boston, but the attention to business affairs was given grudgingly, and whenever forced to be away from his beloved observatory, Lowell used the mails to deliver a constant shower of orders, comments, suggestions, and complaints to the crew at Flagstaff.

The opposition of 1894 afforded Lowell his first chance to view the mysterious lines on Mars through the clear air of Flagstaff. (Mars is said to be "at opposition" when it is [opposite the earth from the sun].) The *canali* were highly visible, and Lowell and Andrew Douglass succeeded in mapping more than 180 of them, an accomplishment that in itself was enough to justify the money spent on the observatory, at least in the opinion of the jubilant Lowell. He wasted no time; in less than a year his book *Mars* was published and created an instant sensation.

In vivid prose Lowell described Mars as a dying world — a chilly, desertlike planet wrapped in a meager atmosphere, with most of its water locked in the snow and ice of its polar caps. During the long Martian summer (seasons on Mars last about twice as long as they do on earth) the polar cap facing the sun melts and grows smaller, while the area surrounding it changes color — an effect Lowell ascribed to the growth of vegetation.

What of the *canali*? They were not easy to see. Even in the clear air of Flagstaff, it was sometimes necessary to spend many hours at the telescope before being rewarded by a few minutes of perfect viewing. But whenever that happened, the *canali* would flash into sight. Narrow, of uniform width, as straight as though drawn by a ruler, the peculiar markings stretched across the surface of Mars for hundreds, even thousands of miles. Whenever two lines crossed, a large dark spot marked the intersection. At first almost invisible, the *canali* grew steadily more conspicuous as the Martian summer wore on.

To suppose for a single moment that this network of geometrically straight lines could be of natural origin was, in Lowell's judgment, absurd. The true nature of the *canali* was to him startling but obvious: they were artificial waterways or canals, constructed thousands of years ago by the Martians in a desperate effort to stave off extinction as water became ever more scarce and areas of sterile desert grew larger and more menacing on their doomed world.

The lines he saw were not the actual waterways but strips of vegetation 15 to 30 miles wide that formed along the edge of the canals, becoming more visible as the summer progressed. The dark spots at the intersections were oases. The evidence was conclusive: Mars was inhabited by some form of extremely intelligent life.

Lowell's bombshell might have caused no more than a mild

flurry had he chosen to present it in a sedate treatise for scientific circles. Lowell, however, had no patience with technical jargon, and *Mars* was written in the crisp, forthright style that he preferred. It reached a vast audience and took it by storm. Of the thousands who read the book, at least 99 percent were captivated by Lowell's description of the red planet and completely convinced by his logic. Overnight Lowell and Mars became front-page news, and everyone with so much as an opera glass handy trotted outdoors to peer at the sky. H. G. Wells, having made a hit with *The Time Machine* and *The Invisible Man*, eagerly seized Lowell's theory and wrote *The War of the Worlds*. Others followed Well's lead, and generations later we still reap the harvest, as any science fiction fan can attest.

The reactions of the professional astronomers were mixed. Some had seen the canals themselves and went along with Lowell's assertions to the extent of a cautious "maybe." Others could not see the strange markings at all and suggested scornfully that they were either an optical illusion or the result of Lowell's wishful thinking.

Lowell hit the ceiling, feeling much as Columbus would have if the savants of Europe had told him that the West Indies were a fantasy. With icy politeness Lowell demanded to know how astronomers who operated in an atmosphere of perpetual smoke, haze, and humidity could find the audacity to question the observations of dedicated men who had spent hundreds of hours viewing Mars through the purest air of any observatory on earth. The dispute continued hot and heavy in both the press and the scientific journals. Lowell, who never backed away from a fight, answered criticism with logic and biting sarcasm. As he was an artist with either weapon, there were times when his opponents must have felt as if they had been put through a shredder.

The argument followed an undulating pattern for 15 years. During those times when Mars was out of sight on the other side of the sun, the canals were allowed to simmer on the back burner while Lowell and his assistants turned their attention to Saturn, Jupiter, and the rest of the solar system. Then, after an interval of 26 months, another opposition would come due and interest in the red plant would wax to fever heat, with stargazers of every nation peering anxiously through their telescopes, trying, more or less patiently, to catch a glimpse of the elusive canals. Some succeeded; some did not. Lowell, of course, tartly insisted that any failure to observe the canals was due to poor conditions or faulty equipment, and most of the public as well as a number of respected astronomers felt he was right.

After the opposition of 1905 Lowell announced that one of his assistants, C. O. Lampland, had photographed the Martian canals. This was astonishing news because the camera, unrivaled for capturing the faint light of stars a million light-years away, is strictly second-rate for observing planetary detail. Upon inspection the photographs proved to be interesting but not convincing. Any attempt to enlarge them resulted in the loss of fine detail, and on the original plates the diameter of Mars was less than one-quarter of an inch. A few sharp-eyed individuals could make out the spiderweb lines of the canals, but most people could not, and the situation was right back where it had been.

The year 1906 saw the publication of *Mars and Its Canals*, followed two years later by *Mars as the Abode of Life*. The two books were illustrated with photographs, maps, and drawings, many in color, and between their covers was crammed all the information on Mars that Lowell had been able to collect. Lowell's reasons for believing Mars to be inhabited were put forward so persuasively that in 1907 *The Wall Street Journal*, not ordinarily noted for its quick acceptance of radical ideas, asserted that the most important event of the previous year was the *proof* that life existed on Mars.

Both *Mars and Its Canals* and *Mars as the Abode of Life* enjoyed popular success, probably due to Lowell's prose style, which was brisk and vigorous enough to have made the instructions for knitting a sweater interesting. Some of the stuffier critics were inclined to wince at his lack of academic dignity, but Lowell, who believed strongly that science would be made comprehensible to the general public, was not disturbed.

Although Lowell had remained single for a good many years, it was not due to any disinclination for feminine companionship, so no great shock was created when, in the spring of 1908, he married his Boston neighbor, Constance Keith. The couple spent their honeymoon in Europe, and while visiting London, Lowell took his bride for a ride in a balloon.

After the publication of his last popular book, *The Evolution of Worlds*, a new challenge began to capture Lowell's attention. As early as 1902 he had become convinced that beyond Neptune lurked an unknown Planet X, and in 1910 he determined to search for it.

Neptune is a giant planet, so distant it takes 164 years to make one circuit of the sun, and it is visible only through a powerful telescope. It was discovered in 1846 by Leverrier and Adams, who deduced that irregularities in the orbit of Uranus were caused by another planet beyond. Working from that information, they calculated the position of Neptune.

The work of Leverrier and Adams was rightly acclaimed a mathematical feat of the first order, but what Lowell was attempting was more difficult. Since its discovery Neptune had completed barely one-third of its orbit, so Lowell was forced to recalculate the irregularities of Uranus, deduct the gravitational perturbations caused by Neptune, and work with the remainder. This was done before the age of computers, and the calculations became so fantastically complex that Lowell hired no fewer than four mathematicians to work under his direction.

Sporadic efforts to find Planet X had been made from time to time, but in 1914 a systematic search was begun. A section of sky was photographed; a few days later another photograph was taken of the same spot, and the two places were compared to see if one star had moved, just a little. As the photographs took in about fifty thousand stars, searching for Planet X was a good deal like decorating a wall with several thousand thumbtacks and noticing the next day that one had been moved a sixteenth of an inch.

It was clear that, barring a miracle, the search for the unknown planet was going to take a very long time. But Lowell, impatient for results, kept prodding the crew at Flagstaff to keep trying. Perhaps he had a premonition there was little time left. If so, he was right. His death came unexpectedly on November 12, 1916.

Lowell's belief in the Martian canals was never shaken. He was not alone; the names of the respected observers who also saw the canals read like a partial who's who of astronomy: Schiaparelli, Pickering, Flammarion, Douglass, Barnard, Lampland, Slipher — the list could go on. As recently as 1939, Dr. Edison Pettit of Palomar reported seeing 40 canals on the surface of Mars. In 1949 Dr. Willy Ley wrote that as of that date the Martian canals did indeed exist.

They were wrong, of course. The canals do not exist and never have, but it was not until the *Mariner* flybys of 1969 and 1971 and the *Viking* orbiters of 1976 that they were finally and forever laid to rest. Which raises the following questions: What did these reputable scientists see? How could Lowell have been so completely wrong?

We know that the surface of Mars is pitted with craters and valleys, dotted with hills, and marked with dry riverbeds. Lowell and others were catching glimpses of certain features that, seen from a distance of thirty five million miles or more, gave the appearance of straight lines. Oddly enough, the sharpest observers were the ones who were fooled.

Lowell died confident that Planet X would eventually be found, and in this case he was right. Early in 1930 Clyde W. Tombaugh, a young astronomer attached to the Lowell Observatory, was working with a new instrument called a blink microscope. He noticed a moving body in the area where Lowell had predicted another planet would be found. For weeks the observatory staff checked and double-checked and then, on the 75th anniversary of Percival Lowell's birth, announced the discovery of Planet X. Later the new planet was given the name Pluto. The first two letters of the name are the initials of Percival Lowell, and the symbol P/L is a P superimposed over an L. It is ironic that what Lowell saw with his own eyes proved to be an illusion, while his major accomplishment — one of the greatest achievements in astronomical history — turned out to be something he never saw.

The World is Flat

THERE ARE SOME PEOPLE who like to do their thinking for themselves. Proven facts don't mean a thing to such folks when they work their way around a problem and come up with a different answer. Let the authorities try to reason them out of their notion; they won't budge a bit if they are convinced that their own reasoning is correct. Let the neighbors snicker and call them "just a little bit out"; it makes no difference. They see no reason why they should take another's theory when they have worked out the problem and can still confound their doubters with unanswerable questions.

Such a man was "Uncle Joe" Holden (1816–1900), who spent most of his life in Otisfield, Maine. He was a hard worker, a deep thinker, and a convincing orator. Putting these three traits together, he came up with the idea that everyone else was on the wrong track when they said that the world was round. He worked upon that assumption again and again and always came up with the same answer: the world was flat.

Since he had 10 brothers and sisters, he had nieces and nephews galore. Most of them lived near him, and they were being taught in school that the world was round. Folks in the big city of Portland said they knew that the world was round. Someone ought to set them straight. So Joseph White Holden named himself a missionary, with his topic always to be "Why the World is Flat."

Uncle Joe was an intelligent, respectable, hardworking man. At different times he owned three sawmills on the brook that served as the outlet of Saturday Pond and flowed into Lake Thompson. He put in long hours at the mills. His hands were calloused from handling the rough logs, but if he got a call to philosophize, he'd clean up and present his logic before a gathering of people. He could hold his own against a scoffer anyday, too! His straightforward manner and novel reasoning gained him a remarkable reputation.

By the time he appeared at Congress Hall in Portland, he was an important enough personage to be interviewed by a newspaper reporter. He had addressed a full house the evening before, and he felt right on top of his flat world. He told the young newspaperman, "When I got through, I didn't ask 'em to do it, but they took a rising vote and said that I had put out facts that can't be answered, and they all believed that the world was flat, too!"

Then came the question that he was always asked: "How did you arrive at such a conclusion?"

He was waiting for that one. He'd settle back in his chair and say, "Well, now, I've talked with many a sailor and not one of them has sailed far enough to come to the end of the earth. It stretches out and out. "Now the reason they always return to their home port even though they sail out in the opposite direction is because their compass always varies just a dite so they never really sail in a straight course."

At that point the reporter decided to change the subject and asked him if he intended to stay over in Portland for another evening. "I'll stay over if I can get 600 people to come hear me. I'm on my way to put up these now." He showed the reporter the stack of posters he had been carrying under his arm. They read:

WILL WONDERS NEVER CEASE! A MAN WHO KNOWS ALL ABOUT IT WILL PROVE THAT THE WORLD IS NOT ROUND BUT FLAT! HE SAYS IT DOES NOT TURN ON ITS AXIS AND DOES NOT REVOLVE AROUND THE SUN. COMMON SENSE IS A SCIENCE! A NOVEL AND UNIQUE LECTURE BY J.W. HOLDEN OF EAST OTISFIELD WILL BE PRESENTED THIS EVENING AT _____

The blanks were to be filled in with handwriting once arrangements for a new appearance had been made.

Shaking his head in perplexity, the reporter bid the old philosopher good day and returned to the newspaper office, thinking, "Obviously the man is no one's fool. He's keen and alert. It would be a laugh if the old duffer turned out to be right after all!"

Another time Uncle Joe was invited to address the elite patrons of Poland Spring. He was introduced in a serious and graceful manner. *The Hilltop*, a newspaper published at the resort, quoted the master of ceremonies, Edwin B. Hale of Boston: "Mr. Holden, in endeavoring to prove that the earth is flat and non-revolving, will place himself among those enthusiasts of history who have risen in opposition to accepted theories and will, in his own estimation, be classed with Columbus, Galileo, John Brown and scores of others who died in forlorn hope or firm conviction."

Basically, Joseph W. Holden was a solid citizen — a farmer and sawyer. He was a lifelong Republican and strong antislavery man. He dreamed of becoming a member of the legislature, where he could address still another audience, but that dream never materialized.

In 1892 Uncle Joe attended the Maine State Fair at Lewiston. He had a field day for himself, buttonholing people and presenting his philosophy. Those who had already done the fair were willing to stop and listen to the old-timer from East Otisfield; the rest would wander by.

Suddenly Uncle Joe spied a really big fish: Dr. Alfred W. Anthony, a professor at Bates College in Lewiston. If he could be convinced, the philosopher knew that he would be well along the road to success.

Stepping up so as to block the professor's way, Uncle Joe slapped his newspaper on his knee and asked in a voice calculated to attract as much attention as possible, "Dr. Anthony, I suppose you believe that the world is round?"

Caught unawares, the mild professor answered, "Why, yes, I certainly do."

"Well, that is the biggest, most all-fired piece of nonsense in the world! How can the world move about the sun?"

"Really, sir, I must be on my way. I have an important appointment to keep," protested the professor, who had no intention of tangling with a crank.

That didn't make a dent in the flow of words coming from Uncle Joe, who was, as usual, completely carried away by his own fluency.

"Now look a-here," he continued. "There's the sun over there, and here she stays in the south. Well, suppose the earth moves around the sun. When it comes six months from now, she ought to be here, hadn't she?"

"Yes," agreed the professor, "it looks so, but you must pardon me, I must hasten." Wiping his brow, he scurried away.

"There, I fixed him!" he said, looking about at the crowd in triumph. "That there question none of 'em can answer. That's a cracker! It stops 'em every time!"

The next year, 1893, he was at the peak of his powers. He was invited to present his theory in person at the Chicago World's Fair. That made the folks of East Otisfield look at him with new respect. His manner was as plain as his dress and speech, yet he could hold the interest of an audience anytime.

But as the years went by, his clothes became shabbier. There was talk about some slicker tricking him into investing most of his competence in fake stock. One source said that, at the last, he would exist for days at a time on only a few cents.

When well-meaning friends attempted to pry into this business, he would keep his lips locked as tight as a clam. He wanted no pity or charity. He never married, nor did he allow any of his nieces or nephews to concern themselves about him.

When the end came, in 1900, Uncle Joe had one more surprise left. When his will was read, it was discovered that he had left funds to have a monument of the finest Italian marble erected on his grave. There it stands, in the beautiful maple-shaded Rayview Cemetery in East Otisfield. The inscription is his own. It reads:

> Prof. Joseph W. Holden
> Born Otisfield, Me.
> Aug. 24, 1816: March 30, 1900
> Prof. Holden, the old Astronomer
> discovered that the Earth
> Is flat and stationary and
> that the sun and moon do move.

He had the last word after all!

The Baker Brothers Build a Submarine

SOME PEOPLE KEEP a car in the garage, others an eclectic potpourri of lawn mowers, firewood, dogs, and baseball bats. Duane Baker, a 36-year-old chef from Burlington, Vermont, had a homemade two-man submarine in his garage. He called it the *Lake Champ Explorer*.

With a long, yellow snout, plastic bubble top, and pair of stuffy propeller-driven fins, the sub looked like a stunted jet fighter 16 feet long, 7 feet across, and 6 feet tall. The cockpit was just big enough for a driver seated at a control panel and a passenger resting on his knees. Fully loaded, the *Explorer*, designed and built with the help of brothers Elmer and Steve, weighed about 1,300 pounds. It was a wet/dry sub — that is, water filled the cabin up to the waist of the driver. Six hours of air was supplied by scuba tanks stored in the nose and hull. While the sub was capable of diving to the 400-foot bottom of Lake Champlain, the Bakers' air equipment permitted dives only to 85 feet, deep enough to explore shipwrecks, do some salvage work, and maybe even photograph "Champ," the legendary monster of Lake Champlain.

"It would sure help pay for the sub," Steve said.

Building the *Explorer* was Duane's dream. As a boy he built working submarine models and read about shipwrecks, sunken treasures, and Indian caves. Reading wasn't enough, though; Duane wanted to see the underworld firsthand. In 1983 he bought the plans to construct a submarine from plywood and fiberglass. When he ran into construction problems, Elmer, an accomplished welder, offered to redesign the *Explorer* and build it from aircraft aluminum in his spare time. "Otherwise, I was afraid he'd drown," Elmer said.

The trio invested $5,000 and 300 hours building the *Explorer*. Steve and Duane became certified scuba divers. Only Elmer has never ventured into the sub. The water bothers his ears.

The *Explorer* made its first dive in August of 1985 in an abandoned stone quarry. Casual observers predicted it would sink like a rock. The *Explorer* performed like a dream. "I just sat there and floated by," Duane recalled. "It is exciting to see the underworld at four miles per hour."

According to Steve, the biggest problem was licensing the sub. The state had no regulations for submarines. It wasn't until the Coast Guard suggested calling the *Explorer* a "submersible boat" that the Bakers were issued a permit.

So What *Is* the Time?

"What, then, is time? If no one asks me, I know what it is. If I wish to explain it to him who asks me, I do not know." — St. Augustine

DR. DAVID PARK was 15 minutes late to the 1980 winter term seminar titled "The Natural Philosophy of Time" he was teaching at Williams College in Williamstown, Massachusetts. But as he would say, the past and future are part of the present; we all exist in an Eternal Now; and therefore the concept of being late has no meaning.

It was an excuse right out of Park's book, *The Image of Eternity: Roots of Time in the Physical World* (University of Massachusetts Press), which had just been awarded in 1980 the Phi Beta Kappa Award for outstanding contributions to the literature of science. Park also was a member and former president of the International Society for the Study of Time.

As St. Augustine pointed out, time is a slippery subject. As an authority on the subject, though, Park was the Wizard of Hours.

There was, perhaps, another reason that Dr. Park was late to his seminar. He never wore a watch "because it's always telling me that I have to stop doing something that interests me in order to do something else." He was then 61 years old and had been teaching physics at Williams for 40 years. He was a lean, active man, and even when stationary he appeared to be in motion, his sparse gray hair streaming away from his head as if he were facing into a strong wind. When thinking, his face would screw up and he would squint into the distance, the deep wrinkles in his forehead squirming and piling up on top of one another like lines of equations chalked on a blackboard.

The squint was not surprising because when he would think hard, it was often about something nobody had ever seen or ever will see — a great sucking vortex in outer space called a black hole, where time and space seem to reverse their properties, or the unbelievably small elementary particles called quarks, whose behavior appears to defy the laws of nature.

Quarks were the topic of Park's lecture the day he was late, but he got off the track and started talking about Einstein and the German mathematician Werner Heisenberg, whose theories about the nature of the universe, he said, had helped to kill common sense. By "common sense" he meant our perceptions of the world based on direct experience, "the physics we learn at our mother's knee." Up until this century all of physics had been built upon a foundation of common sense. Then Einstein and Heisenberg came along and declared that common sense was not correct. It was good enough to get by with in our daily lives, but when applied to objects enormously large or incredibly small, it fell apart.

Sometimes Park's lectures were hard for ordinary people to follow. The only way to describe or explain a black hole with any accuracy is mathematically — trying to put it into words changes the meaning. Words are based on common sense, which is outraged by black holes, quarks, and the theory of relativity.

At his next class that day, Park talked about the geometry of the black hole, a collapsed star in which the atoms are so tightly packed together that a teaspoonful of its substance would weigh many tons. This terrific density and mass so warps the fabric of space and time that they appear to reverse their functions, he said. Time in a black hole would be measured with a ruler, space and a clock.

Then he touched on a theoretical model of how time would be distorted for a space traveler (hypothetical, of course) going from the center of a black hole (known in physics as "the singularity") past its boundary with ordinary space ("the event horizon") to a point several thousand miles away and then back again. The space traveler leaves the singularity at 11:30 A.M. He crosses the event horizon billions of years in the past. He arrives at the point several thousand miles away at 12 o'clock noon on the day he left and turns around to go back. He recrosses the event horizon billions of years in the future and arrives at the singularity one hour after he left it.

"Are there any questions?" Park asked the class. Nobody had understood him well enough to have any.

Park traced his New England ancestry to Sir Robert Park, one of Governor Winthrop's advisers, who left Boston to make what was called then "the long walk through the woods" to the Connecticut River, which he descended, settling in Saybrook, Connecticut. David Park also was fond of long walks. He was planning a trip to the Himalayas to walk around Annapurna, the world's seventh highest mountain. He also described a trip he took with his son the previous summer in which they walked across the Pyrenees from Spain to France. "It was all snow from eight thousand feet up," he said. "We had to carve each footstep very carefully or take the chance of sliding all the way back down."

Science is something like that, Park explained. People tend to think of scientists making giant leaps of imagination, as Einstein did with relativity, when actually science "is a process of taking the smallest, most conservative steps possible, all along the way."

To a listener, that seemed hard to reconcile with black holes and quarks. It seemed like an example of complementarity, the term physicists use to describe a situation when two theories, each one experimentally provable, contradict each other. Is light made of waves or particles? You can use experiments to prove it is made of waves. You also can prove it is made of particles. Language again. Park quoted Danish physicist Niels Bohr, who said there are two kinds of truth, trivial and profound. The opposite of a trivial truth is falsehood. The opposite of a profound truth is another profound truth.

Complementarity fit into Park's theory about the nature of time. There are two times, he said, Time 1 and Time 2. Time 1 is the time measured by a clock, the time of physics, moving persistently from past to future, in which there is no such thing as now. Time 2 is the time of human consciousness, the Eternal Now, in which past and future are contained. "We all experience Time 1 and Time 2," Park mused, "but only alternately. It's difficult to imagine experiencing both at the same time. I am either living in the present moment, Time 2, or I have somehow stepped back from the present into Time 1 to consider the past or the future."

Park's wife used to say that he floated in time. "She can remember exactly when she studied certain subjects in school," he said, "while I haven't the remotest notion. And when I try to remember exactly when some event occurred, I'm likely to be as much as ten years off." Perhaps it was because he preferred to spend most of his time in Time 2, "caught up in the headlong present."

For all that, though, Park did not consider himself a specialist in time. The subject, he claimed, "takes up only a fraction of my time and attention. Einstein used to complain that he had spent by far his greatest amount of time and attention on quantum mechanics but was forever being asked about relativity."

Perhaps, then, David Park was not the Wizard of Hours after all. He mentioned the founder of the International Society for the Study of Time. "He calls us the Friends of Time," Park said, "but I think he is more than than. I think he is a lover of time."

Dr. J. T. Fraser, a short balding man with gray hair and glasses who lived in Westport, Connecticut, said he preferred to be thought of as "the best friend of time." The best friend of time was born in Hungary in 1923, and his consuming interest in the subject began during World War II, an event that disrupted his life and the lives of millions of others, "People have often asked me if I had some kind of curious visitation from heaven, or from outer space, that suddenly interested me in time," he said. "The answer is no. If one is in a very bad position, as I was during the war, and all you want to do is survive a little longer, perhaps for another couple of days, you can't help but think about time. Not because of anything supernatural, but because of the nature of what we are."

After the war, Fraser found his way to New York, where he paid his way through college by selling hot pastrami sandwiches at a place call Dirty Joe's. Then he worked as an engineer, specializing in magnetic resonance and the design of antennas. "It had a fascination for me, and still does," he recalled.

"People become so blasé. They say it's just an antenna. But the antenna is what connects a tangible object — a radio, say — with the intangible. From there on, things just go somewhere. I can't touch a radio wave. I can't feel it. The antenna is just at the edge of emptiness."

Fraser enjoyed his work as a scientist, and he won several U.S. patents. But his first love was time, and in 1966 he published a collection of original essays on the subject from a wide variety of contributors. He called the book *The Voices of Time*, and on the same day it was published he founded the International Society for the Study of Time. By 1980 it included 120 members, all accomplished scholars, from 30 nations. Fraser acted as the society's secretary, and he was listed on its letterhead with 10 other members of its administrative council. Under each name was the discipline in which the members specialized — physics, English, history, music, biology. Beneath Fraser's name it said "The study of time." He had done nothing else for the preceding 10 years, and so far as he knew, there was no other person in the world with the same full-time occupation.

Fraser wrote books and articles about time, taught college courses as a visiting professor, and lectured to interested groups ranging from the American Psychoanalytic Association to patrons of the Metropolitan Museum of Art. When strangers would ask him what he did, he would size them up quickly. If they appeared to have no real interest in his work, he'd tell them that he made fittings for hydraulic pumps, which tended to discourage further inquiry.

But if they seemed genuinely interested, he'd tell them the truth and watch their reaction. It served as what he called "a temporal Rorschach [inkblot] test." Most people would react in a way that could tell Fraser a great deal about them. "If I were to say that I study some kind of Indian tribe, they would say, 'That's interesting,' but they would not be surprised. When I say, 'I study time,' they are surprised that anybody should be interested in it. What is there to be said about it?"

"But it has another, deeper level," he went on. "When I say *time*, I name a concept that is emotionally loaded. For some people, time is no more than what the clock measures. But even for them as for all of us, consciously or unconsciously, time is a reminder of our passing, of opportunities lost, of the precious quality of minutes that came and went, a reminder of death. Like everything else, it is a mystery."

There was a certain air of mystery about Fraser, too — an almost secretive quality. He would never discuss details of his wartime experiences. He allowed an interviewer to use a tape recorder, but then used a tape recorder like a time machine — abruptly turning it off, rewinding to the beginning of a sentence or phrase he had thought better of, and recording over it — editing and censoring the interview as it took place.

"One cannot really talk about time in the same way that one talks about a table," Fraser said. "Time, as a concept, as an experience, has to do with the fate of man — perhaps the destiny of man.

"On the other hand, the knowledge of time is closely tied to the knowledge that we are going to die. And although animals do show a mortal terror before an imminent danger, there is no evidence that suggests that animals ever think about death or their fate. It is only man who does that. Perhaps it robs us of an ability to enjoy our lives. But in the opinion of many artists, writers, and philosophers, it is the knowledge of mortality that makes us human, makes us able to appreciate the present."

The present was the province of Dr. R. Glenn Hall, chief of Scientific Operations for the Time Service Division of the U.S. Naval Observatory in Washington. The Wizard. If you were to ask him what time it was, he'd say, "We make it. . . . Well, we determine it — from the stars and from atomic clocks."

Stars and clocks don't quite agree, Hall said, but the difference is very small. Eastern standard time, (EST) for example, is very close to, but not identical to, mean solar time. That is, the sun can't reach the zenith at precisely 12 o'clock noon in both Boston and Detroit. The sun keeps moving. Or rather, the earth does. Measuring time by the sun and stars is really using the earth as a clock, and the fact is that atomic clocks are more accurate than the earth. The earth's rotation is slowing down by almost a full second every year. So in 1972, Hall and his colleagues around the world started compensating for it by adding a "leap second" to the end of every year.

It took three years, from 1955 to 1958, to calibrate the first atomic clocks. They are extremely accurate, losing about a nanosecond (one billionth of a second) per day. "It might be a little bit more or a little bit less," Hall said, "but how can we measure it?" Like the antenna, the atomic clock is right out there on the edge of emptiness.

You can learn the exact time by calling a special number at the U.S. Naval Observatory (202-254-4950), which will give you EST in hours, minutes, and seconds after midnight and the Universal time — known to most of us as Greenwich time — which is EST plus five hours. "It's as exact as we can make it," Hall said with reassuring confidence. "Of course, by the time you hear it over the phone, it may be off by a tenth of a second or so."

But is it *really* the right time? Isn't it just something that we all sort of made up? "Yes," said Hall. "But it's the convention we have agreed upon, so we know it to be true."

The Mother of Mulch

"I'VE BEEN LIBERATED FROM BIRTH," Ruth Stout said when in her mid-nineties, "and gotten away with it, too."

Best known for her gardening books and as a columnist, lecturer, teacher, and sometime philosopher, Ruth explained her independent spirit at her rural Connecticut home of half a century. "I'm normal enough to be pleased if a person likes me," she said, "but I wouldn't squander a penny for anybody's approval."

The lifelong attitude of following nobody's rules — "not even God's" — without giving them some thought almost landed her in jail — once when she was a teenager growing up in Prohibition Kansas and again after she turned 90.

"I was just sixteen when Carry Nation came to Topeka to do some barroom smashing," Ruth says, explaining her first brush with the law in 1900. At dawn, on a Sunday morning, "Carry smashed one plate-glass window, and I smashed the other." Feeling very noble, Ruth anticipated going to jail with the famous prohibitionist. "But I didn't make it. They arrested Carry, led her away, and ignored me! I went to Sunday school instead." In her later years Ruth would have an occasional brandy. "Pardon me, Carry," she would say, raising her glass.

Ruth Stout was a bit of a rebel all her life, but her nonconforming attitudes kept her ahead of the times in many ways. In 1930 Ruth moved with her husband, Fred, to a 55-acre farm, in Redding Ridge, Connecticut, and began homesteading. Several years later she pioneered an entirely new way to raise vegetables that thousands of gardeners across the country adopted. Her revolutionary approach used a deep, year-round mulch on the garden, eliminating plowing, harrowing, hoeing, weeding, watering, fertilizing, poisoning, or cultivating — in short, eliminating work.

"Gardening, like anything else," Ruth said, "shouldn't be so much work that one can't enjoy it." To Ruth, gardening was a personal adventure. "It's a little bit like cooking," she said. "Read the recipe and then use your head. A dash of skepticism can do no harm. Go lightly on caution, heavily on adventure, and see what comes out." Of her many books, two of the best known, *How to Have a Green Thumb Without an Aching Back* and *Gardening Without Work*, became bibles to homesteaders and suburban gardeners alike.

Ruth lived alone after her husband died in 1962. She was self-reliant and, well into her nineties, continued to plant (with a little help from a friend) the many vegetables and herbs that were the mainstay of her larder. She ordered staples by mail and froze her vegetables for use during winter months. "I haven't been in a supermarket in over fifteen years," she remarked at the age of 95.

Since she'd published her first article in 1953 and *Organic Gardening and Farming* magazine had listed her garden as one of "Fifty Places to Visit" in 1956, Ruth Stout had become a legendary figure, the "Mother of Mulch." In the late 1970s, a New York filmmaker produced a film about Ruth and her garden, and each spring she was inundated by requests to speak at garden clubs about her laborsaving methods. But her appeal wasn't limited to gardeners. She offered sound alternatives for nearly every aspect of life. "Planning a garden," she would say, "is like planning a way of life. Arrange it to please yourself, copying neither convention nor tradition nor any individual."

Those fortunate enough to have visited Ruth's no-work garden came away with more than a look at newly sprouted peas or a taste of parsley. Simplicity was the key to her garden and to her life. Famed fellow gardener Scott Nearing once said of her, "Ruth Stout is proof that a person can live a happy, sane, and simple life in a mixed-up world."

Ruth's 300-year-old house was Spartan in its furnishings but had a pleasant, lived-in look. There was an old-fashioned coffee grinder in the big country kitchen, along with an eye-catching basket of squash from the garden. In the living room were several comfortable chairs, a sturdy worktable, and a few Oriental prints on the walls. The wide floorboards were bare and the windows curtainless. Ruth chatted with her visitors in 1979 from a faded couch beside the stone fireplace, mixing her gardening lore with personal reminiscences.

Like her garden, the house required no heavy work. This gave her more time to pursue other interests, including writing. She had nine books published and mailed off her tenth manuscript shortly before her 95th birthday. Titled *Don't Forget to Smile*, it was a book containing some of her "mind cures" and exploring the relationship between one's mind and body in the treatment of illness. She attributed her longevity to the power of positive thinking ("If you expect to have something wrong with you when you begin to get old, the sad part is that you probably will"), exercise, heredity, and good food ("Food is cheaper than a doctor and more enjoyable"). But Ruth didn't often stress the healthful factor of organic gardening. "It doesn't seem necessary to tell people that eating poison isn't a good idea. I should think they know that. Besides, people don't like to be told what's good for them, do they?"

Her near century of originality was been celebrated in *I've Always Done It My Way*, a book written "to prove I never had problems because I didn't follow the herd." Born in 1884 on a Kansas farm to Quaker parents, Ruth was one of nine children. (Her brother Rex Stout, also an avid gardener, was the creator of the orchid-loving Nero Wolfe, hero of a series of detective novels.) "Mother was used to crazy goings-on and had a habit of letting everyone follow his own inner light without any remarks from her." Early on, Ruth adopted that kind of thinking for herself.

"Before I reached my teens, I had quite a list of things I planned to do to make me famous," Ruth said. Acting and writing headed the list. Her early short stories appeared regularly in local Kansas papers. printed under a pseudonym. "This way I got honest opinions on the stories—never mind if I didn't always like them." In high school she went on the road with a fake mind-reading act. Although this vaudeville performance was short-lived, it fired her ambitions and prompted her trek to New York in 1908.

Since acting jobs were scarce in the city, she tried her hand at a variety of occupations. She sold some stories to pulp magazines (one poem titled "Three Kisses" earned her three dollars); she worked as a bookkeeper, a telephone operator, and an office manager and eventually opened up a Greenwich Village tearoom. "There was a customer who came into the tearoom one afternoon and liked the place so much she came back that evening and brought her husband, Fred Rossiter," Ruth said. "That was a mistake from her angle," she added, laughing, "because Fred and I fell in love with each other."

When Fred's wife wouldn't give him a divorce, Ruth stopped seeing him for seven years. She became active in leftist causes, working as business manager for the *New Masses* and arranging debates among noteworthies such as Scott Nearing, Clarence Darrow, and Bertrand Russell. She took a year off to do famine relief work with the Quakers in Russia (where she promptly gave away all her clothes). Then back in New York, while distributing *New Masses* at a lecture, she had another mild flirtation with the law. When trouble was anticipated during the political meeting, she couldn't resist showing two very surprised police officers her small suitcase. She told them, "This has my nightgown in it, in case you take me to jail." She wasn't arrested. "Lucky for me — I was just faking."

In 1929 she married Fred Rossiter, retaining her maiden name for her work. A year later they dropped out of New York and "retired" to rural Connecticut. Ruth was 45; Fred was 47.

"It isn't surprising that at our age Fred and I had opinions about the ridiculous promise to obey, love, and honor one another," Ruth said. "You can obey, I suppose, but then loving and honoring go right out the window and you're incapable of stopping them." Accordingly, their marriage was full of invention, teamwork, and the undisputed right to pursue their own interests. For Ruth that meant gardening, and it wasn't long before she was fully convinced she had discovered something important. Soon she was writing and lecturing about her antitraditional methods. When scientists and "experts" questioned her, she met her critics head-on and became a spokeswoman for the "lazy gardener's" approach.

Fred was once asked how he could retire at age 47. "It's simple," he said. "I married a woman who doesn't want anything." Ruth put it another way: "I abandoned *dollars* in favor of *hours*."

"I was lucky to meet Fred," Ruth said, "because not many men would have put up with the out-of-order things I always did." There were the years she gardened nude because she liked the feel of the sun and air on her body. "Do you know what my attitude was? Well, they don't have to look if they disapprove, but if they do want to look, let them!" Then there was Ruth's total disregard for fashion. She wore shorts into town long before that was an acceptable practice for women. She outlined the shape of her foot and asked a man to make a pair of shoes for her. "But lady, nobody would wear a shoe like that," he said. Ruth did. She managed to earn praise for a fashionable dress she wore on television's "I've Got a Secret," only to tell her admirers she was glad they liked her dress — she had enjoyed it herself for 30 years.

"Fred once said about me, 'Ruth may not have a green thumb, but she has a green tongue.'" As she was saying, she'd been liberated from birth.

2

ARTISTS

The Mountain Carver

"BORGLUM IS ABOUT TO DESTROY another mountain. Thank God it is in South Dakota where no one will ever see it."

That was the opinion of one newspaper writer when sculptor Gutzon Borglum, inventor of the monumental art of mountain carving, announced his plan to carve the figures of four U.S. presidents in the granite of Mount Rushmore. He had developed and perfected his technique of mountain carving at Stone Mountain in Georgia, where he planned and partially completed a monument to the Confederate Army. For Mount Rushmore the obvious choices were Washington, Lincoln, and Jefferson, but Borglum's decision to carve Teddy Roosevelt, an old friend of his, drew some skepticism.

"He made our dream come true by completing the Panama Canal," Borglum said.

"And he looks like you," the critics countered, "except he has more hair. Are you sure you aren't trying to put yourself on the mountain?"

Perhaps he was, Gutzon Borglum was always a figure larger than life. Born in an Idaho log cabin in 1867, he left home in his teens, determined to be famous before he was 30. He studied sculpture in France with the great Rodin and returned to become a sensation in his native land. His *Mares of Diomedes* was the first American work purchased for the Metropolitan Museum of Art, and his huge marble bust of Lincoln is a permanent exhibit in the U.S. Captiol.

But Borglum's dreams, opinions, and ambitions were too vast to be confined to art. His friend Supreme Court justice Felix Frankfurter wrote, "Gutzon loved wars, a whole lot of wars, six wars at a time." He was an active campaigner for Roosevelt's Bull Moose party and a leader of the Connecticut Progressives. In 1918 he took on the Wilson administration with his aircraft industry investigation that uncovered widespread corruption. He started a fight club in New York that resulted in the legalization of boxing in that state. He helped draft a constitution for the new Republic of Czechoslovakia and made his estate in Stamford, Connecticut, a training ground for a 3,000-man army of Czech legionnaires.

Borglum's first Mount Rushmore figure, that of Washington, was unveiled on Independence Day in 1930. He lived to see his critics silenced, but he died in 1941, before the great project was completed. It remains his monument — one that, as he said in a typical burst of enthusiasm, "will outlast our civilization."

JOHN MASON

The Coffin Builders' Art

Long after supper on May 19, 1900, a rain-soaked reporter walked into the city room of the old *Boston Journal* and sat wearily down at his desk. He was hungry and tired. All day he'd been tramping around the neat little town of Wilmington, Massachusetts, talking to the undertaker, the coachman, and the relatives, friends, and neighbors of Mrs. Frances B. Hiller — the magnificent Mrs. Hiller — whose death had brought crowds of curious people to Wilmington.

From four o'clock to six o'clock on that rainy afternoon hundreds had filed through the front parlor where Mrs. Hiller lay in her $30,000 casket, clad in a silk robe that cost $20,000 and surrounded by costly floral tributes — one a clock made of blossoms with the hands pointing to quarter past six, the hour she died, and two snow-white doves with outspread wings on top.

As he thumbed a waterlogged notebook, the reporter scowled again and shoved his eyeshade high on his head. "Hey Boss, how do you spell sarcophagus? You know, the big carved box they put the casket in?"

In Wilmington there had been much speculation over Mrs. Hiller's funeral. Would it, people asked, be as elaborate as she had planned? Would her costly casket actually be borne through the streets on a huge funeral car with a 19-foot canopy? Was it true that she was going to wear all those rings and diamonds?

Way back in 1873 there arrived in the town of Wilmington, a young doctor and his wife by the name of Hiller — a name that will never be forgotten in the town. Henry Hiller was born in Mannheim, Germany, and got his doctor's degree there. He moved to England and married a charming young English woman who had just graduated from a London medical school. They took a honeymoon trip to America and liked it so well they settled on Cape Cod. But after a while Dr. Hiller felt they could better serve humanity and themselves if they were near a big city. So they came up to Boston and looked around for a future home. The town of Wilmington appealed to them, and there they settled, building a big new house of 14 rooms near the railroad station.

Dr. Hiller had invented a patent medicine (or elixir), and he sold a lot of it in his office on Tremont Street in Boston. He got rich very fast and was free with his money. To a *Boston Herald* reporter Mrs. Hiller said, "Everything we touched turned to gold in our hands. We were as happy as could be save for one thing. Children were born to us, but they did not live. Though we both were vigorous, our little ones pined away and died in early life; so of the 23 darlings I have borne, 14 of whom were twins, not one is alive today to give joy to my heart and add sunshine to my home. It was God's will. Let his will be done."

Besides being interested in art, music, and science, the Hillers were interested in spirituality and often talked of the hereafter.

Mrs. Hiller, who loved things costly, elaborate, and bizarre, said she wanted a casket such as had never been seen before, and the doctor agreed that they couldn't spend their money in any better way.

Over in Cambridge lived a very famous wood-carver and cabinetmaker by the name of James MacGreggor, and to MacGreggor the Hillers went with their plans and specifications. The grand old Scotsman listened open mouthed as the doctor and his wife described the two caskets and the inner box that they wanted built and decorated. He figured and figured and finally told them that even with the help of his four expert assistants, it would take at least seven years to do the carvings. But if they would pay him $40 a week, big money in those days, he would go ahead with the job.

The original coffin was to have been for Mrs. Hiller, but it was the doctor who died first — on November 7, 1888, after having been thrown from his carriage. Just two weeks before his death one of the neighbors had asked him how his casket was coming along. He replied, "Oh, it'll be ready when I need it." But it wasn't half finished when death came, so his body was placed in a vault in nearby Winchester, and the funeral was postponed until the following year.

On the first of September 1889 MacGreggor announced that the first costly coffin had been completed and he was ready to tackle the second one. Mrs. Hiller announced that the doctor's funeral would be held in a few days, on September 4, which it was.

Three and a half years later MacGreggor finished the second casket — an exact duplicate of the doctor's. When it was delivered to Wilmington, Mrs. Hiller was so proud of it she had it set up in the front parlor. When her friends came to call, she would climb in and lie down so they could see "just how splendid she would look when she was all laid out."

The outside casket was supported by eight heavy brass lion's paws. They were 17 inches high, cost $100 apiece, and weighed 475 pounds. When the steel hammock was hung inside the inner box (and that was placed in the outside casket) and the lion's paws were put under the whole affair, it stood 5 feet from the floor and weighed a little over 2,000 pounds! It was said to have cost close to $30,000.

The cover of the casket had two ivy vines running around the edge, meeting in the center, where there was a skull carved in wood. A lizard was creeping out of the eye socket in the skull. But that wasn't all. On the ends and sides of the casket MacGreggor and his assistants had carved angels, cupids, and dragons by the dozen. There were bats flying over serpents and a big owl holding a tiny field mouse in its talons, all carved in mahogany four inches thick.

Inside the box a metal hammock was suspended from the four corners of a second inner chamber, and on the cover of this box were gold and silver plates engraved with portraits of the doctor and his wife and their 23 children.

In describing the caskets they had ordered, Mrs. Hiller said, "I paid over $1,000 for planks from the giant redwood trees of California, but they weren't good enough and I cast them aside. Then I paid $2,000 for some cedars of Lebanon and discarded those."

Mrs. Hiller was no piker when it came to spending her money after the doctor passed away. She planned a mausoleum 40 feet square and 40 feet high, with plate-glass windows behind a bronze grating so that visitors could come and look at the costly coffins and fancy carvings. "Two watchmen," said Mrs. Hiller, "will be on guard day and night, and there will be lights burning as long as the world lasts."

Five years after Dr. Hiller died, friends and relatives of Mrs. Hiller were startled when they received bright red invitations printed with gold ink that read as follows: "You are cordially invited to be present at the renewal of marriage vows of Frances B. Hiller and Henry Hiller, at their residence at 2 P.M., Easter Sunday, April 2nd, 1893." The townsfolk were flabbergasted. Just how could the comely widow renew her marriage vows with Henry Hiller when he had departed this earth five years before? And why wasn't he referred to on the invitation as *Dr.* Hiller?

Well, here's what happened — in Mrs. Hiller's own words to the society editors of that day. "Among my servants," she said, "there was Peter Surette, my coachman. He came from Montreal, and he was always a perfect gentleman. One day Peter asked me if it was true that I was going to marry again, and I told him 'no.' He seemed very happy, and shortly thereafter he began his lovemaking.

"'I'm a poor servant without money or friends,' he said, 'but I am a faithful, devoted admirer of your womanly qualities, and, as humble as I am, please consider a proposal from me.'

"I was thunderstruck at first, but the subject attracted my attention, and I said, 'Why not?' He is honest, loyal, obedient, and loving. I remembered how some of the greatest men of our time came

The Coffin Builders' Art

33

from the meek and lowly, and began to make inquiries. Father Ryan consulted Peter and told me that Peter did not love my money but me. I then found out that he came from a very good family and would be a good man to look out for my property. Accordingly I asked him if he was willing to sign the antenuptial settlement, and he wanted to know what that meant. I told him, and again he expostulated that it was not my money he was after, but he loved me as only man can love. I shall have him placed in the hands of a tutor and fitted for Harvard."

The second Mr. Hiller promptly applied himself to the task of educating himself (although the Harvard idea didn't work out) so as to be properly fitted to occupy the place in society to which he had been elevated. So in 1893 — five years after the death of Dr. Hiller — they got married. But instead of Mrs. Hiller becoming Mrs. Surette, she had her husband's name changed (by a special act of the legislature) to Henry Hiller — and Henry Hiller he was to the end of his life. (He outlived Mrs. Hiller by more then forty years.)

Mrs. Hiller's romance and wedding were the sole topic of conversation for months, eclipsed only by the funeral that she had elaborately planned years before her death.

Every reporter who could be spared was in Wilmington covering the grandiose funeral of the glamorous Mrs. Hiller, who died at age 56 on May 18, 1900, after a long illness. Early in the morning, workmen took down the wooden casing around the private vault in back of the Hiller homestead and wheeled out the two ornately carved, massive sarcophagi and placed them on the lawn. A big crowd gathered, hoping to catch a glimpse of the rich carvings on the costly caskets, but only a few reporters and relatives saw the owls, angels, birds, and snakes that had been painstakingly carved in the solid mahogany 12 years before. The warm spring sunshine glistened on the solid brass lion's paws at the four corners of the heavy boxes. A special patented lifting device was brought from Boston to lower the boxes into the tomb.

The mammoth funeral car (designed by Mrs. Hiller and specially built long before her death) was so high it would not go under the trolley wires, so carpenters hastily cut it down 14 inches. It was, in reality, more of a truck than a car and was most impressive, completely covered in black velvet with broadcloth draperies sweeping the curbstone. Mr. Charles Nichols of Woburn was seated in a big chair on the truck from which he drove the four coal-black horses caparisoned with black netting.

The *Boston Traveler* reported that on the day of the funeral, May 23, "thousands crammed the trolleys and steam cars — and hundreds of others blocked the side roads with carriages and bicycles."

The procession formed at 9:30 — an open landau filled with flowers, then the hacks all drawn by black horses. It took ten men to lift the casket through the side windows, and, when they rested the coffin on the veranda railings, the supports buckled. A number of the bearers scrambled down the steps and hastened to the lawn, where they put their shoulders under the case and sustained its weight. After a brief rest, they took their burden to the rear of the funeral car and zigzagged one end of the case up to the floor of the somber canopy. As the casket rested upon the car, there was a moment of intense excitement. The canopy on the car, which lifted its top 19 feet above the street, swayed alarmingly, and the body of the car settled and lurched as if about to collapse. After a few minutes' effort on the part of the bearers, the casket was moved to the center of the car's floor.

During the transferring of the remains from the house to the street, cameras were used on every side. The heavy breathing of the bearers and the click of the "snap boxes" were the sounds that punctured the impressive silence. (This was one of the first funerals to be covered by news photographers.) Hats were raised and heads were bowed by a few who stared in wonder as the strange though much-heralded exhibition passed as if it were a holiday review. Henry Hiller rode in the first of the eight carriages in the procession.

The fences along the street and in front of houses served as seats for the curious. The highway was blocked with people. Trains whizzed by the little railroad station near at hand, and passengers craned their necks from the car windows. They had evidently planned to see as much as possible of the spectacle during their flight through the village.

After the service, the sarcophagus was rolled into the tomb beside that of Dr. Hiller, the massive gates were closed, and everyone thought that the two famous Hillers would always remain in the mausoleum. Early in June 1935, however, the 10-foot-high tomb at the entrance to Wildwood Cemetery determined to be an eyesore. So it was decided to level the ground and put the caskets in the ground. It was quite a job, and the workmen dug for several hours. When the pick of one of the workmen struck the grave, there was a loud "whoosh." The workmen dropped their tools and ran away, frightened. But it was only the air coming out of the tomblike vault.

The caskets were in excellent condition, and none of the carvings had been hurt by being buried. The caskets were lowered from the tomb into the ground, and there they are today with no stone to mark them.

MATHEW D. BEEBE

King of the Cowbells

Dressed in tails and top hat, the Great Dr. Casey begins. "Probably the best place to play the cowbells is in heaven, but I better play them now because there's liable to be so few of you there," he says, chiding the audience, members of the American Bell Association. Looking back across his shoulder he asks his band, "What do you say we play a little music for the folks here?"

"Yeah."

"Are ya ready?"

"Yeah, we're ready!"

"Well, let's go, then!"

A piano bangs out a rough accompaniment. The Great Dr. Casey grabs a bell, shaking it only for a moment, switching to another and then another. He moves frantically about the table, grabbing and ringing bells, just keeping them in time with the piano. He's playing a song, "Blueberry Hill," as it has never been played before — with a set of cowbells, the finest collection of antique cowbells in the world.

The Great Dr. Casey was not really a doctor. His band was nothing more than his own voice, taped precisely to allow colloquy between the doctor and himself. He was a doctor only in the sense that on the day of this 1982 performance he was very probably the leading antique cowbell expert in the world. The Great Dr. Casey was James M. Whitney, then 82 years old, of Nashua, New Hampshire.

Jim Whitney looked younger then. He could have passed for a man in his sixties — lean, with bright, cheery eyes and an angular face. Snowy-white hair and full dark eyebrows offset the eyes and sharp nose, and a pencil-thin mustache, barely noticeable, graced his upper lip. He lived alone in his home on a small rise overlooking Fifield Street in Nashua, where he was born and raised. He was the self-proclaimed "King of the Cowbell Carillon," with an infectious smile and endearing personality.

In 10 years, Whitney had amassed a collection of more than one hundred bells. Though he admitted to having collected "quite a few clinkers," the cream of the antique crop was a 35-bell carillon of cowbells, the finest of the bells Whitney had found. Each cowbell sounded a chord, not just a single note, and the collection was arranged chromatically, covering nearly three full octaves. He was proud to say that to his knowledge, "it is by far the best set in the world." The "clinkers" went into a special box, a graveyard of poor-sounding bells that didn't measure up to the finer-toned bells in the collection. Whitney's musical ear was very good, and he could instantly discern a cowbell's chord by matching the strike tone (the dominant note) to a note played on a harmonica or piano.

Jim Whitney found new additions for his collection by touring flea markets and garage sales. He had a few favorite stops where his luck was a little better than at others, but mostly he drove around scouring each place for a low C needed to complete his three octaves or a high-pitched bell to improve his assortment. Collecting cowbells often proved to be expensive. He paid as little as 25 cents and as much as $18. When he was lucky enough to find one, Whitney would shake the bell, then pinpoint the note on a harmonica he always carried in his pocket. "I usually attend a dozen or so flea markets a year, sometimes two or three a month at least. And I ring every bell."

Hunting through flea markets increased Whitney's addiction to collecting, which came to include old bottles and construction tools ("I'm a sucker for buying anything."). He was a refined and polished pack rat, in that most of the many objects he collected had a practical use or were rare, extraordinary, or unique. Undoubtedly his largest collection was kept under a tape recorder in his vastly overcrowded living room, where he had stacked thousands of pages of sheet music. "And I don't collect many construction tools, just when I see a good piece at a flea market," Whitney said. 'But I have a few props and things from when I used to entertain more."

"A few" is somewhat of an understatement, considering the props he had found from bygone entertainment days — the era of traveling shows and $40-a-week wages. Some still worked, including a contraption that simulated a lion's roar, a ratchet, and whistles that created lifelike cow, rooster, train whistle, and other sounds.

As an entertainer, Whitney appeared on four radio shows, doing comedy or playing his banjo, and was a guest on the *Johnny Carson Show*, but he most enjoyed his days as a drummer with the Gus Hill traveling minstrel show. He was a member of the touring minstrels in 1920 when they followed Al Jolson on a Canadian tour. His show days ended when he settled down to raise a family, but his affinity for entertainment endured. The butterflies fluttered and his throat seemed parched before the cowbell performances of his later years.

The show was indisputably a novelty. Whitney admitted that once you'd seen it, you were not likely to see it again. But if you saw and heard it once, the faint clanking of cowbells would be with you forever.

A Singular Life

YOU STAND THERE FEELING SAD as you read the lettering on the tombstones: "Poor dear little heart . . ." "Oh, how I feel for her . . ." "She was a cunning little heart . . ." Ages four, nine, and over twelve. Youngsters brush by you to get a glimpse of what you're reading and give a sigh of sorrow. Then a placard nearby catches your eye and turns your gloom into mirth. Its message reveals that the epitaphs and the stones are a memorial by Miss Nancy Luce, who wanted to immortalize three of her favorite hens.

The two stone markers with three inscriptions may be seen at the Dukes County Historical Society building in Edgartown, Massachusetts, with chiseled-in verse of what Nancy Luce thought appropriate for "Ada Queetie," who died in 1858, "Beauty Limma," who died in 1859, and "Tweedle Dedel Bebbee Pinky," who died in 1871.

Miss Luce was born in 1811 in West Tisbury, Martha's Vineyard, Massachusetts, and devoted most of her life to the raising and pampering of her pets, mostly chickens, treating them almost as her equals. When they died, she put them in little coffins and, with great lamenting, buried their bodies in a graveyard that she had set aside in her yard. When Nancy died at the age of 79, in 1890, there were some 35 pets in her homestead cemetery.

As a result of her odd ways, some folks, mostly from off the island, called her the "chicken woman," "chicken crazy," "light-in-the-head," and "eccentric old maid," among other names. But little did Nancy care, if she heard what they said, for she went right on nursing and tending her brood.

In fact, Miss Luce capitalized on what other people thought

were her shortcomings. She had a flair for showmanship and eventually attracted many visitors, some distinguished people of the day, to see her home where her chickens roamed about freely. She charged an admission fee and offered photographs of herself and her pets for sale, as well as handwritten verses of "poetry." She was an exquisite penwoman, writing with neat Spencerian scrolls, carefully forming each letter, a style that was perhaps perfected to make the selling of her poems more attractive to visitors.

Apparently her verses were a hit, for in 1860 she had them published in a little booklet, which was followed by several more editions, the last of which was printed in 1898. Occasionally a copy can be found in some bookshop.

There was a rumor that Nancy's spinsterhood was the result of her suitor's leaving the island on a whaling ship and never returning. For a time a huge whalebone believed to be a gift from her lover was displayed in her yard. Her writing gives no indication that she was ever jilted.

One of her earliest pets was a goat that Nancy tenderly cared for until it died at 10 years of age. Throughout her life she kept a cow for milk. She wrote, "Milk agrees with me, other victuals distress me . . . I must have milk to live on or go without eating 'til I die."

The idolizing of her chickens became a mania. She would talk to them and give them special foods. In the wee hours of cold winter mornings she would make sure the fire was burning briskly in her rooms to keep her flock warm. If one of them became ill, she was like a fanatic until it was nursed back to health. "I never took off none of my clothes for 18 days and nights," she wrote after bringing one chicken through a sickness.

"Ada Queetie," she wrote, ". . . knew every word I said to her. She would do 54 wonderful and cunning things." This included shaking the bottom of Lucy's cape with her bill when told, scratching the back of Lucy's hand, and shaking "hands."

All of her hens were given names made up of an odd jumble of syllables and letters that apparently meant something to Lucy. Some of the names recorded in her writings are Feleanyo Appre, Letoozie Tickling, Teedie Tealy, Mealeny Teatolly, Speckeket Lepurivo, Kalally Roseiekey, Levendy Ludandy, and Jantie Jafy, plus those on the headstones mentioned above.

To reward Nancy Luce for her kindness, the hens would lay a bounty of eggs, more than "anybody's hens anywhere," she wrote.

The name of each hen was recorded on the eggs she laid, and often Nancy would keep the eggs much longer than she should have. Some of the eggs were sold to help support her home.

Nancy kept meticulous records of many transactions and gave specific instructions when she ordered supplies from the mainland. In a request for fuel she wrote, "2 barrels of coke, cole, that sort the kerosene is all took out of it."

She acquired such a reputation for nursing sick hens back to health that many of the island folk brought their birds to her for advice or to see whether she could cure them. In her booklet she told about "Hens — Their Diseases and Cures." One of her favorite remedies was Epsom salts and black pepper. She claimed she cured Tweedle Dedel Bebbee Pinky of distemper with this concoction. She sat up with this ailing hen one night until 11 P.M., and when it seemed better, she put it on "a good soft bed" and lay down beside it, talking to it all through the night. In a few days, she wrote, it "got well and smart."

Olive and castor oil also could cure many things, she said. If a hen had a "warped neck," her instructions were to give it "a little Huile d'Olive to take inside; a good chance her neck come in place again." It also cured one of her hens of a "swelled head."

It was believed that when Nancy was about twenty years old, her health began to fail. She complained in her writings of her ailments, which were thought by some to be largely neuralgia and loneliness. "My head [is] a place of misery at all times," she wrote, ". . . rheumatism from head to feet." Her records include many purchases of medicine.

Although she must have been aware of the joshing about her, she showed little ill will toward humanity in her writings. She did refer to antagonists as "hard hearts" and "murderers," but her booklet dwelled for the most part on her pets, with sprinklings of religious thoughts and her condition of health.

She wanted her pet cemetery to be guarded with caution. "I am in fear," she wrote, "that some two-legged satan will go there at night and break my dears' little gravestones to bits."

In her final will and testament, which was probated April 21, 1890, at Edgartown, she bequeathed her cow and hens to a neighbor. "And I request," she willed, "that as soon as I die he chop off the head of every one of my hens, quick and short, and put them out of misery quickly. They must suffer no sufferings nor be cruelled in any way, nor mourn for me. This must be seen to."

It was her wish at one time to be buried in the cemetery with her pets and for the remains of her favorites be put in her coffin with her. Close friends finally convinced her that this was not wise, and today she lies in the West Tisbury Cemetery.

EDIE CLARK

Hartford's Historian

THE WIND BLEW THE SNOW across the intersection in sheets. It was February 8, 1945. Tony DeBonee was at the corner of Main and Pearl streets, the windiest place in all of Hartford. He wanted a picture of the snow, one that would show the feeling of people struggling against the wind. He had his camera in his pocket. He was the only person out. He waited. He was barely into his twenties. He wore no gloves, he wore no hat. He rubbed his hands together and blew into them. He needed someone in the picture. Come on, someone! Ten minutes passed. A half hour passed. No one came. Forty-five minutes. He hopped up and down. After an hour he spotted a woman coming down Pearl Street, her umbrella filled with wind, the snow swirling around her like a veil. Bless you, lady bless you! Tony took his camera out of his pocket and squinted into the viewfinder. The umbrella moved into the center of his scene. *Click.*

Tony got his shot in the blizzard, as he has continued to do ever since. Tony Debonee became a historian, a Hartford historian, though he didn't have a lot of degrees. In fact, he never went to college, but his high school diploma was hung on the wall of a busy cafeteria in downtown Hartford among a sampling — that is to say, dozens, including the one taken in the 1945 blizzard — of his photographs. His kind of history.

Tony DeBonee was always crazy about Hartford. He started out collecting postcards — only Hartford scenes — when he was 10. After a while he decided he could do it better himself. So when he was 19, he bought a Brownie box camera and started snapping. That makes 1942 the beginning of recorded history for Tony and for the Hartford Historical Files Society, of which he was founder, president, and sole supporting member.

Even at that age it was for the record. His mother had given him a few old family photographs. "But she never had enough," he explained. "All they did was pose and pose and pose. They didn't show a trolley car or an aeroplane or the old nickelodeons. You never knew what it was really like." That was his mission, to show what it was really like. His photos, especially the early ones, are alive with street scenes and horse-drawn milk wagons and workers on strike and celebrations at the end of the war — anything so long as it was Hartford.

Tony was a small, wiry man, a coil of energy, with brown eyes and thinning brown hair that was usually covered by a fedora worn at an angle. There was something faintly musical about him, as if, walking down the street, he might suddenly do a quick tap dance. He spoke quickly and sincerely in a tough, gravelly voice, a little like James Cagney. On his fingers he wore rings, gem-studded rings, that glinted as he smoked his cigar. "My only fault," he would say.

In his later years he lived in East Hartford, over the line, out of bounds, in a pink house down a narrow side street that represents the only time he lived outside of Hartford, where he spent nearly all of his life. "I've lived all over Hartford — the North End, up in the Mark Twain area, in three different places on Park Street. I lived on Main Street, yeah, all over." He went over into East Hartford because it was cheaper but also because it gave him some rest.

"When I'm in Hartford, all I want to do is take pictures," he said.

The house was jammed with negatives and photographs and collections of Hartford memorabilia — and a camera on the kitchen table. "Here's my famous little camera," he told a visitor in the late 1980s, picking it up and holding it in his palm. It was a Kodak Instamatic, then the latest in a lengthy line of cheap cameras. "I got it for fifty cents at a flea market about twenty-one years ago."

Tony only took the pictures. He never had a darkroom and didn't know the first thing about that part. "I leave that to the experts," he said. Neither did he have any instruction. He learned as he went along. "I never had any money in those days. I just had money for film, so I'd buy a cheap camera, and when it broke, I'd go get another one. But this is my favorite," he said of the battered little box. "It's the one I carry with me all the time. Now, why do I need an expensive camera? It would just be stolen."

The negatives made by the cheap cameras were in file drawers, cross-referenced with the prints and the contact sheets that were in other file drawers, and the slides were in another cabinet altogether — numbered, dated, categorized. The slides were newcomers to the historical record. "What happened was a woman sold me a roll of film for slides, and I didn't know it. So I went around taking pictures, I got them developed, and they came back as slides. I liked them! So I said what the heck, I'll take slides, too."

Some of the files he kept in his bedroom, which he called his office or, sometimes, his arcade. There he had pinups and pictures of all his children, his old girlfriends, his first wife, his second wife, and his favorite singer, Deanna Durbin. In the kitchen, bottles and mugs and jugs, anything that was made in Hartford, lined the walls and cupboards and windowsills. He displayed some of his favorite photographs in the dining room, which served as his gallery. It was an exhibit that he would often change depending on who was coming to visit. The tops of the two sideboards, on either side of the table, were loaded with frames propped side to side, no room for another. And the walls were so tightly hung with pictures that there was hardly a line in between that showed the plaster. The dining room table was covered with plate glass, under which he would slide his newest favorites. "There would never be space to show them all," he said, somewhat superfluously.

The living room, however, showed astonishing restraint. The pink wallpapered walls were bare. "I try to keep Hartford out of here," he said. There was one exception. In the corner, next to the divan, a big framed collage displays the faces of eight tender newborns, with the dates of births marked next to each, 1959 to 1967. "These are all my kids. This is why I call this my family room." He thought a minute. He couldn't help it. "They're all born in Hartford hospitals! All Hartford products!"

In the basement, though, the theme picked up again — more files, more scrapbooks. And the shelves of what was once a root cellar were packed solid with his collection of different editions of *Huck Finn* and *Tom Sawyer*. Tony didn't see the need to point out that Mark Twain lived in Hartford. Everybody knows that. And, in the corner, he had his brick collection. Bricks from the dozens of buildings that have been demolished in Hartford during his lifetime. And a cobblestone from the rail yard before they tore it up. This also was history to Tony. "The history that took place on top of this cobblestone, you know, you just couldn't record it," he said, hefting it like a gold bar.

But these other collections were momentary fascinations, most likely taken up when the light was too dim to take pictures. More than anything else, his pictures were his record. And it was only in his mid-sixties that he began showing his pictures to anyone but his family. "I did it for my kids. I wanted them to have this after I'm gone." In spite of himself, his pictures were discovered, and people started to call and write to ask for copies. "For forty-three years I was well hidden," he said in 1987, still surprised. "Somebody discovered me, and it's been crazy ever since." He didn't charge people who wrote asking for prints. "If they send me a few extra bucks, it's nice; I can use it for film. But I'm not a professional. I'm the common man's amateur photographer."

It was kind of a snowball. Two brothers, Bob and Dave McKay, were looking for pictures of "old Hartford" to put up in their Main Street restaurant, the Municipal Cafeteria. They heard about Tony from a friend of a friend and went all over to find him. They finally did, and he was so pleased to think that someone else would enjoy the pictures that he gave Bob and Dave armloads of pictures and memorabilia, including his diploma. The old pictures drew a lot of attention; people wanted to know where they came from, and the Hartford *Courant* found out and did a piece on Tony. "That's me! In the paper!" he said, showing a visitor a clipping that he had preserved in a plastic casing. The library found out, too, and put up an exhibit that stayed in the lobby for several months. That's when the phone calls started — because what his pictures showed were what it was like.

They were not art; they were not perfect. Tony was the first to admit it. "I don't use any lighting. I don't use any props. Everything is hand held and trust to God that He gives the light that I want." But Tony figured out what was so special about his pictures. "In my day, there weren't too many people walking around with a camera. Today everybody's got a camera. And yet very few people carry the camera around with them. The only shots in their scrapbooks are in the backyard or at the beach or at a graduation."

Tony spent a lifetime recording the city as it changed. He showed up at dedications for buildings, ground breakings, demolitions. He used to go up on roofs of buildings — go up fire escapes to get to the top. A lot of those buildings were gone in 1987, and there wasn't a fire escape in sight. "But I've got a record of all of them! I had some lean years, you know. I had two marriages and eight kids, and there were some rough times. When the kids started coming along, it got a lot harder to go out and take pictures. But every once in a while I'd sneak into town. But then I was single again, and I'd take snowstorms, and when St. Joseph's caught on fire, the smoke was still there when I got there. Then there was the strike at Pratt and Whitney, and I took pictures of the ambulances when people got hurt, and I went up in an airplane and took pictures up there. I was on my way again."

There was another marriage and another round of kids. "That slowed me down again. But here's what I did. I started the Hartford Historical Files Society. It's newspaper clippings, things about things I couldn't go out and take pictures of. Even when I was tied down, I made sure I never missed a thing."

One sunny day in 1987 Tony took a guest along on one of his jaunts. There was always plenty he could show someone from out of town, since even people who lived in town didn't know the city the way Tony did. The night before he had made up a list of the places the tour would include. He had the list on a clipboard under his arm as he locked the back door. And he had his camera. "I'm armed!" he said, patting the pocket of his trench coat. "And plenty of ammunition," he said, flipping a yellow film packet from out of his vest pocket.

Tony drove a gold Lincoln Continental Mark V, a car whose

front seat was so big and so plush that when he got into it, pulling the armrest out from its concealment, it was like he was settling down into an easy chair. "This is a vintage car. That's why I love it. It's ten years old and built like a tank." He put the clipboard on the dash for easy reference.

He maneuvered the car out into the narrow street. The big, wide fenders moved ahead like guardian angels, all but grazing the sides of cars parked on either side. Tony didn't notice; he was talking about how much the city had grown in recent years. "Hartford, Hartford. When I was growing up, it was always the same, nothing changed—nothing doing for years! Then, all of a sudden, boom! It's almost more than one man can keep up with. I try to cover everything—I read the paper, word of mouth, everybody is always telling me about something that's going on, so I write it down on my schedule and try to get there."

Tony figured that at that moment there were eight projects going up and four in the planning stages. "I've got all these sites photographed from the ground up, every step, so that if I was to flip the pictures fast in front of you, you'd see the building go right up."

To get into Hartford he had to go out onto the interstate, and as he came off the exit ramp into the city limits, the cluster of Hartford's high buildings popped into view. "You're coming into the skyline. When I was a little boy, there were only three buildings that stuck up—the Travelers, Hartford Bank and Trust, and G. Fox. Look at this now!" The tall, glassy new buildings reflected the sun, a dazzling sight. On the edges, giant cranes hoisted steel girders and buckets of cement up onto new frames. "Sixteen square miles—I don't know how much more they can do. They'll have to move out."

He turned into downtown Hartford, busy with rush-hour traffic. The sun rested on his face. His eyes were turned upward. He pointed. "See this white building over there—looks like paper clips or hairpins. Isn't that beautiful? That's the Hartford Square North going up."

He turned a few more corners. "There's the boat building—the only two-sided building in the world! They call it a boat because it's set into a pond, like a moat or something." It looked like a boat, with glass from the top of its tall height all the way down to the street.

Many of his early photographs were taken on the street. He

didn't take random snapshots on the street so much in his later years. He found that it had its dangers. He was once chased for four blocks by someone who wanted to know why he was taking his picture, and his car had been stoned going through different neighborhoods. "And I don't like to see my car banged up, you know? So I have to pick days that are crowded. When you go in on a weekend, when it's quiet, all of a sudden, boom! Rocks and whatnot. But — it's the hazard of the trade."

He cruised through a red light, majestically, as if making a conquest. A horn sounded. "No problem," he said. He was concentrating on the buildings. "Every building has a history, believe me. And every street has a history."

He pointed to a side street. "There's Park Street — my favorite street! That's where I grew up."

He pointed out the place where the floodwater had come up to the steps of the meetinghouse and the cross on top of the steeple on St. Joseph's Church, which he said he rubbed for good luck before they hoisted it up. He drove slowly past the Colt factory, with its peculiarly Mideastern onion dome, painted blue and gold; and the stilt building, which Tony circled twice for a good look at its spidery supports; and the gold building, which Tony particularly liked to photograph when the sun hit it and made the buildings around it shimmer with watery sunlight; and the home of one of Tony's heroes, the man who invented the Gatling gun. He passed an old boarded-up factory near the railroad tracks. "See that window right there? My mother waved to me from that window when I went to war."

At the Comet Diner he made a note on the clipboard to come back and take a picture. He never took a picture haphazardly. He studied each site, noticing when the light would be right. "It's pretty hard to find something that I haven't got pictures of," he said. The Comet was one. It used to be the Aetna Diner. "I asked my first wife's father if I could marry her in there. It's pretty hard to photograph because the sun doesn't hit it 'til late July. But it's on the agenda. Yep, I want that one."

He made a left, past the Mark Twain House. "We're heading into Katharine Hepburn territory," he continued. She was another of his collectibles. A picture of her was under the glass of the sideboard in his dining room. "This is the end of the Nook Farm, where all those literary characters lived." He motioned to a parking lot, girded with a chain-link fence. "Right where these cars are parked is where Katharine Hepburn's house was."

He drove past the Royal Typewriter factory, where he spent more than eight years putting together typewriters; past Kane's brick factory and the Heublein factory, where they made vodka; past the Fuller Brush building, where brushes were no longer made. He had pictures of all of these.

He swung onto Prospect Street, the city line. The other side of the street, East Hartford, was no-man's-land. "I only look at this side of the street," he said, pointing to the Hartford side. "I have to limit myself, believe me; otherwise it would be endless."

He drifted through another light that had turned red. An oncoming car swerved.

Tony was starting to feel hungry and headed back over to the center of town to the Muni, where he was as regular as the guy behind the counter. The Muncipal Cafeteria was starting to crowd up, and the dishes clattering and the rising conversations made it hard to hear Frank Sinatra singing in the background. There were old pictures everywhere. Many of them were Tony's. He loved the way people enjoyed the pictures at the restaurant. "I don't ask for anything. I want the people to enjoy them. I'm happy just to have them know I took the picture. They say, 'Hey, you took that picture?' and I say, 'Yeah!' "

From up front Tony got a roast beef on a hard roll and a coffee and took a table in line with the door so he could see who was coming and going. A man with snow-white hair and a bright red scarf around his neck came in. "Hey, Bob!" Tony called out.

Tony greeted Bob Echelson, who took off his scarf and sat down next to him. Like Tony, he had lived in Hartford all his life but found it a bit dull. Bob looked at Tony. "What's so great about Hartford, Tony?"

Tony was silent for a minute. Finally he said, "I don't know. If I had been born in Boston, I would have been crazy about Boston, because this is my nature. It's my heritage, that's what I love — where I was born, where I went to school, where I was married, where all my kids were born. For me it's always been Hartford, Hartford. But if I moved to Boston or some other place now, no, it wouldn't have that attraction. I haven't got that long to live! I'd still continue on with Hartford. I'd still get the Hartford *Courant*. This is a lifetime."

He got up from the table. From the pocket of his trench coat he drew out the camera and walked backward, eyeing Bob sitting at the booth. He bent his knees a little bit, brought the camera up to his face, his elbows out like wings, and said, "OK, nice smile! Thatsa way!" and the flash popped, a brilliant light in the midst of the lunchtime crowd, circa 1987. Tony's kind of history.

3

Performers
and Prodigies

MICHAEL BURKE

Tallest Lady in the World

IN 1888 A WOMAN NAMED Sylvia Hardy died. The world took little notice of the event, and both the fact of her passing and the character of her life have almost vanished from record. But Sylvia had been famous once: she was the "Maine Giantess," touted by P. T. Barnum as "The Tallest Lady in the World."

The Lewiston *Journal*, in 1869, reported that at age 46 she was 7 feet 10 ½ inches tall. At her death she weighed about 400 pounds. She may have been the tallest woman in the world during her life-time, and she was easily the tallest woman ever to have been born in the United States up to that time.

Sylvia was indeed a giant, yet she was also a person — a woman, daughter, and friend. How hard it must have been for people of her time (and even our own) to see beyond her giant shadow. It must have been just as difficult for Sylvia herself.

In the century since her death three women have taken an interest in Sylvia's story and tried to preserve it. The first was Lena Adams, whose husband, Harry, was a grandnephew of Sylvia's. Much of the family memorabilia was passed down to her, and she in turn passed it on to Blanche Applebee, a schoolteacher and writer from North Jay, Maine. In the 1940s and 1950s Applebee gathered what stories she could from the few persons still alive who had known or seen Sylvia and from contemporary newspaper accounts. Before her death in 1985 she turned her material over to Maxine Scott of Wilton, Maine, who thus became the unofficial historian of Sylvia Hardy. If not for the efforts of these three women, Sylvia's story might have vanished forever.

Sylvia was born on August 17, 1823, in Wilton, a little town on the shore of Wilson Pond, midway between Rangeley and Lewiston, north and south, and Farmington and Rumford, east and west. Her father was John Hardy, son of William, one of the early settlers in town, and her mother was Jane Dalley. Sylvia was the first child of the Hardys, and she weighed but five pounds at birth. Apparently she had a twin brother who died at four months, and according to the wisdom of the day this accounted for Sylvia's eventual size — she having "taken" the growth from her twin. Sylvia's father died when she was seven, and her mother married Benjamin Leonard and was widowed by him, too.

Sylvia's early childhood was essentially unremarkable. Giants are not born, of course, nor are they created in one spectacular burst; they result from growing at an abnormally rapid rate, a process that may continue into their thirties. Sylvia started her schooling when not quite 3 years old and didn't take on any noticeable size until she was 12. She went through a stage of tremendous growth then, and at 18, weakened by the unnaturally swift changes, she broke a hip and was in bed for two months. Thereafter she walked with a stooping gait and was always slightly lame. A picture of her taken about this time shows an attractive, stylish woman who was rather sober faced with a set, down-turned mouth and a thin scarf wound and knotted around her head.

As a young woman Sylvia worked "out," which in those days meant lodging temporarily with a family to assist during an illness or after the birth of a child. By all accounts she was an uncommonly good nurse, particularly because she could hold a baby entirely in one hand — the baby's head resting on her fingertips and its bottom on her wrist — while doing housework with the other hand.

Her life seems to have proceeded in this fashion through her twenties and thirties, still growing, working in neighbor's houses, and living with her widowed mother. She might have remained a local oddity if it hadn't been for a fellow named Leon Bump, who lived in Wilton at the time. Leon had a cousin from Middleborough, Massachusetts — Lavinia Bump — who was a midget, standing 31 inches tall. In 1863 Lavinia married the famous "General Tom Thumb," Charles S. Stratton, also a midget, who was the star of P. T. Barnum's American Museum in New York City. Lavinia used to visit Leon in Wilton, and it was inevitable that the tiny lady should be introduced to the giant one. So it was in the spring of 1871 that Sylvia was persuaded to leave her home and her mother and join Barnum's New York show as "The Tallest Lady in the World."

Like many other questions about her, the question of Sylvia's actual size is now impossible to answer. Barnum, of course, exaggerated it, just as he introduced Charles Stratton to the world as General Tom Thumb, declaring that he was 11 years old and an Englishman, when in fact he was only 6 and from Connecticut. George Goding, who as a boy in 1880 boarded with Sylvia and her mother while he attended school in Wilton, claimed that Barnum had Sylvia wear built-up shoes and striped dresses to make her look even taller.

Still, the height of 7 feet 10½ inches seems to have been accepted by many witnesses. The Portland *Argus* reported that at age 30, Sylvia was 7 feet 6 inches, weighed 300 pounds, and was still growing. In addition, one of the few surviving photographs of Sylvia, taken while she was with Barnum, distinctly shows that she suffered from acromegaly, a progressive enlargement of the hands, feet, nose, lips, tongue, and lower jaw, which, while not the result of giantism, is caused by an irregular pituitary gland, as is giantism. One of Sylvia's dresses, owned by the Wilton Historical Society, measures 6 feet 8 inches. Add 10 or 12 inches to account for her head and neck and take away a few to allow for Barnum's platform shoes, and it seems safe to say that she was well over 7 feet tall.

She was on exhibit for 10 weeks in New York, then went with Barnum when he turned his museum into a traveling circus touring New England and the West. The show traveled in large coaches over rough, rutted country roads. On these journeys General and Mrs. Thumb would get tossed about so badly that Sylvia would take one in each hand and support them until they were over the worst parts.

At the end of her brief career with Barnum, Sylvia traveled for a time with a Colonel Wood, who had a show that toured the United States and Cuba, then she returned to Wilton to the house on Depot Street she had bought for her mother and herself. There she began another chapter in her life. At the same time she had joined Barnum's show, she had developed an interest in the "science" of spiritualism. She decided that she was a medium and that it was her task to convert all the world to spiritualism.

She held séances in her house nearly every night for the last fifteen or so years of her life. These were open to anyone she could get to come, although most of those who attended seem to have been young local men. Participants remembered that she would all but drag people off the streets to have enough gathered around the table for the séance.

One person recalled how spooky these sessions were, with a giant invoking the spirits who would respond by means of thunderous raps on the table. Apparently it was a regular occurrence for the table to lift itself off the ground, drawn to Sylvia's hands, which she held a few inches above its top. Harry Adams, her grand-nephew, recalled one famous incident in which several men took hold of the legs of the table and tried to prevent it from moving around the room. In one version of the story the legs of the table actually came off without inhibiting its wild dance. "There was something about the way that table seemed to fight back — exactly as if you was wrestling with something alive," Harry said. Adding to the strangeness of the scene was the reported fact that Sylvia's hair-pins would pop out of her hair during the séance.

Otherwise she lived a quiet and mostly healthy life in Wilton until the arthritis that typically accompanies giantism finally crippled her a few months before her death. The front door of her house, along with part of the side paneling, had to be removed to get the eight-foot-long casket out of the house on rollers. Sixteen pallbearers couldn't lift it. She was buried in the Weld Street Cemetery in Wilton but was moved later to the Lakeview Cemetery overlooking Wilson Pond. It was said that the reason she was moved was because some of her spiritualist friends had heard that she wasn't resting comfortably.

Surprisingly, there is little mention in Sylvia's history of the taunting to which she must have been subject. A contemporary historian, John Haven Willard, writing in *The Maine Farmer* in 1867, mentions a man unexpectedly encountering Sylvia on a sidewalk in Wilton and leaping six or eight feet sideways in amazement. Blanche Applebee tells a story she heard from George Goding, the boarder. It seems a traveling salesman was staying in Sylvia's house one night and began to make remarks about her size. While the other boarders tried to sidetrack the conversation, the city slicker wouldn't leave her alone. Finally Sylvia, who had been ignoring the man, reached across the table, lifted him straight out of his seat, and slammed him back down through the cane bottom, all without saying a word. The boarder remained silent for the remainder of the meal.

Another popular story is of a time when Sylvia was working in a farmer's home. While carrying two full quart milk pans into the house, she got her hair caught on an iron hook that hung from the ceiling. Unable to set the milk down to free herself, she called for help. The farmer came but delayed freeing her while he called for others to come and see her fantastic predicament, whereupon Sylvia poured the contents of both milk pans over his head.

If the reaction of others to her was unusual, so too was the manner in which she lived. In her house on Depot Street the shades were set six to eight inches below the tops of the windows, so she could see out. She kept her looking glass and hairbrush on the top ledges of the windows, alongside photos tacked to the ceiling of her friends from the Barnum days. When she left the show, Barnum had given her a gold watch that measured five inches in diameter, the size of a tea saucer. It was said that a ring she wore was big enough to serve as a child's bracelet. Neighbors reported that her windows were decorated with black cats, in keeping with her spiritualist beliefs.

Apparently her Barnum years (no one, not even the Circus World Museum Library in Baraboo, Wisconsin, could say how long she appeared with his show) were the happiest of her life. Having been thrown together with other people of extraordinary proportions or features, she found in some sense her peers and made perhaps her only true friends. A photo album (since lost) containing pictures and postcards of the other side show performers was one of her cherished possessions, and each card was signed with a token of affection for Sylvia. These friends included the India Rubber Man, the Wild Men of Borneo, the Living Skeleton, the Bearded Lady and her son the Dog-Faced Boy, the Siamese Twins, and of course, General and Mrs. Tom Thumb. Her favorite photo was from Mrs. Thumb and was inscribed, "To my best friend, Sylvia, from her best friend, Lavinia."

Friends must have been exceptionally important to her, as it takes little imagination to see that hers was a life of great loneliness. Her predecessor as the Tallest Lady in the World, Anna Swan, married another giant, Captain Martin Van Buren Bates (making them the World's Tallest Husband and Wife). But Sylvia had no such companion. Indeed, her mother's wish was to outlive Sylvia, presumably to provide her with companionship. She just barely made it; Jane Hardy Leonard died two weeks after her daughter.

To describe a giant, we emphasize the grand details: the head brushing the ceiling, the spread hands that could cover a newspaper, the difficulties of living in an ordinary-sized world. To describe a person, we need the more modest details of character. It is these small details that are missing from Sylvia's story. Those that survive suggest a kind of average person trapped in a body that must have seemed a cruel mistake. She was said to be a good cook. She grew flowers, visited neighbors, and went for long walks in the woods and fields. She used to fashion doll clothes and bonnets for neighborhood children and swap posies with their mothers. Sometimes she would pass out flowers to the children passing by on their way to school.

Comments that describe her as other than a giant or a spiritualist are rare and not very helpful. Her "eyes were as black as soot," said one. "She had thick, black hair," remarked another. Several people mentioned that she was masculine looking and had a deep voice. A woman who sang at her funeral remembered that she "talked very intelligently." The Portland *Argus* disputed the color of her eyes, saying they were blue, but otherwise noted that "her complexion is fair . . . and the very modest and mild expression of her countenance is said to be the index of her character."

As she grew helplessly from the rather attractive young woman with the scarf in her hair to the acromegalic giant whose eyes sank into the flesh of her face, she must have come to see it as punishment. It isn't too much to imagine that her fascination with the spirit world, and with her own death (her coffin had been ready for 10 years by the time she died), suggest a hope for a better world, or at least a different one, in which she'd be free of the sentence of her size. Perhaps the best indication of how she felt about her life as a giant is the brief inscription she ordered for her tombstone. She had once been famous as the Maine Giantess and the Tallest Lady in the World, but on her gravestone there is only the simple message: "Sylvia Hardy. Died August 25, 1888. Aged 65."

MARIA DABROWSKI

General Tom Thumb

IN THE MID-1840S nearly everyone in the world had heard of General Tom Thumb, and today, a century and a half later, his name lives on. No other midget has so captured the public's imagination or achieved the fortune and lasting fame of little Charlie Stratton, born in Bridgeport, Connecticut, in January 1838. What lies behind his unusual fame? Probably these two factors hold the answer: first, P. T. Barnum's tremendous flair for showmanship, with the important element of perfect timing, and second but no less important, Tom's wit and piquant personality as a child. Barnum's choice of the name General Tom Thumb was another stroke of Barnum genius and must have contributed heavily to the child's success.

Had Barnum been content with merely exhibiting the Little General in his American Museum in New York, it is doubtful that Tom Thumb's name would have become a household word. What made him a world sensation was the glamour that surrounded him. Audiences before the kings, emperors, and queens of England, Russia, France, Spain, and Belgium made Tom Thumb the pet of London and Paris society and furnished him with beautiful costumes, jewels, and his own small fine carriages made by the queen's carriage maker in London. Everyone wanted to see the miniature child who had charmed the queen of England, but when they saw him, they fell in love with him for himself, for Tom Thumb had a roguish, saucy way that was endearing.

Except in size, Charles Sherwood Stratton was a normal, healthy child. There was no deformity of proportion; he was a beautifully formed miniature with golden hair, rosy cheeks, and a quick wit and intelligence. At age 4½, when Barnum took him over, the Little General was only 25 inches tall and weighed 50 pounds; he had stopped growing at age 5 months. Years later, at about age 14, he resumed growth and eventually reached a height of 35 inches. The Stratton's had two normal daughters older than Tom and, many years later, a normal son.

Tom's father, who was a carpenter by trade, was bitterly ashamed of his tiny son. Mrs. Stratton was a cleaning woman at a Bridgeport tavern, the Sterling House, and often carried her little boy to work in a market basket. He was a pet of Mrs. Fairchild, wife of the tavern keeper, and it is she who brought Tom to the attention of Barnum's half-brother, who ran the rival Franklin House.

When, through a delay in transportation, Barnum was forced to spend a night in Bridgeport, Mrs. Fairchild, dressing the child in a blue velveteen suit she had made for him, arranged an interview with the showman. (Although Barnum was reasonably successful and very well known at the time, it was actually through Tom Thumb that he found his later great success and fortune.) Barnum was enchanted with the tiny boy and induced his mother to go to New York with him on a four-week contract at three dollars a week. Barnum says in his memoirs that he had no idea at the time what a gold mine he was acquiring.

Mrs. Stratton and Tom arrived in New York in November 1842. Barnum hired a tutor and a dancing master for the child, but he himself coached Tom afternoons and evenings in jokes, verses, and skits. The amazing 5-year-old prodigy was ready for his debut only two months later. Barnum advertised him as an English import, 11 years of age. The performances, three a day with many private appearances in the evenings, were a game to the child. He strutted about in a pert and impish way, exchanging quips with the audience, and overnight became the darling of New York. Fashionable carriages lined the street outside the museum, the papers were full of him, and his picture was in every shop window. At the end of the four-week contract, Barnum raised Tom's salary to $25 a week and later to $50. After two years, following the first European tour, the Strattons shared equally with Barnum in the immense profits. To give an idea of the earnings, a day's average was $500; on one of Tom's later European tours his share was close to $1 million.

At the end of the second year, after a tour of the Eastern Seaboard, Barnum decided it was time for a European tour. The day they sailed, 7-year-old Tom Thumb performed at the museum until

11 A.M.; the boat sailed at noon. More than eighty thousand people had stormed the museum to see him; ten thousand turned out to see him off, and he was escorted aboard by the City Brass Band.

Despite his mother's presence, the tutor, and the dancing master, it was hardly a healthy environment, and certainly not a normal one, for a child. It is small wonder that at 20, Tom Thumb was jaded and world-weary. Consider this schedule for a child of 7, according to the New York *Evening Post* of January 16, 1844: "A few hours more remain for General Tom Thumb to be seen ... as the packet in which he was engaged passage to England does not sail today, in consequence of the easterly winds now prevailing. He may be seen throughout the entire day and evening and at three and seven o'clock P.M. there will be grand performances."

In the Barnum group sailing to Europe were Tom and his tutor, Mrs. Stratton and her husband, who would act as ticket taker, and Barnum. After a stormy 19-day crossing they landed at Liverpool. Barnum had planned to go at once to London to try to present Tom Thumb to the queen, knowing that a command performance would establish them securely. But upon arrival there he learned that the royal family was in mourning, and although it was not impossible to gain an audience, doing so was much more difficult. Barnum plotted his coup d'état cannily. He rented a furnished house in the most fashionable part of Mayfair and from his social stronghold issued invitations to a series of receptions to members of the nobility and London editors. Horace Greeley, one of Barnum's close friends, had given him a letter of introduction to the impeccable Edward Everett, American ambassador to the Court of St. James. Barnum says in his memoirs that it was to this letter he owed his ultimate success in getting Tom before the queen and so launched to fortune.

While impatiently awaiting the audience, Barnum finally decided to show Tom to the public. He hired Egyptian Hall, and besides daily appearances there, the child gave many evening performances at houses of the nobility. His first patroness was the Baroness Rothschild. Everett finally arranged a meeting at his house between Barnum and Mr. Murray, master of the royal household. At this Sunday breakfast Barnum dropped the hint that the General was about to go to France to see Louis Philippe. Murray rose to the bait and assured Barnum that Her Majesty would like to see Tom first. The day of the command performance Barnum, publicity wise, had a placard placed on the door of the exhibition hall: "Closed this evening, General Tom Thumb being at Buckingham Palace by Command of Her Majesty." From that time on, the pounds, shillings, and pence rolled in like a tidal wave.

One of the most beguiling and wistful portraits of Tom Thumb as a child can be found in Barnum's description of this first of three royal visits. Barnum had been instructed that under no circumstances were they to address the queen directly and that they must at all times face her, so that when they left her presence, they must back out bowing. The queen and a large family group awaited them in the royal picture gallery. Tom Thumb trotted smartly down the long gallery, bowed solemnly, and piped directly to Victoria, "Good evening, ladies and gentlemen!" The queen was enchanted by the child's simplicity and took his hand in delight to lead him about. Tom informed Her Majesty that he found her paintings "first-rate" and told her he should like to see the Prince of Wales. The queen regretted that H.R.H. was in bed (where the Little General should have been) but invited him to come again to meet the prince. (Years later, on a trip to New York, the future King Edward looked up the Little General.)

After an hour's performance in which Tom Thumb danced the hornpipe, impersonated Napoleon, sang several songs, and posed as Grecian statues, backing-out time came. Barnum, six feet two, managed well, but poor Tom's little legs were unable to keep up, and when he saw Barnum yards behind him, he turned and ran a few steps, quickly faced the queen, and bowed low in respect, continuing by this method to reach the end of the long gallery. This time Vicoria was "amused" but not so her pet spaniel, which dashed for the General's legs. The terrified boy raised his tiny malacca cane and thrashed out at the dog while everyone there went into gales of laughter. Victoria sent Barnum a bag of gold coins and sent Tom, a pearl bibelot ornamented with emeralds, her first of many gifts.

After tremendous success in England Barnum took the General to Paris, where he was presented many times to the royal family. Tom Thumb became the rage of Paris as "Le General Tom Pouce," and a smart new café was named for him (whenever you have a Pouce-café you are toasting little Charlie Stratton of Bridgeport). Aside from his regular appearances, this amazing child soon appeared in a play, *Petit Poucet*, speaking his part in French!

The General became a familiar sight on the streets of Paris in his five-foot-long carriage. It was drawn by four matched ponies, and on the box sat two small children dressed as coachman and footman in sky-blue livery trimmed with silver lace, cocked hats on their powdered wigs. As the carriage rolled down the Champs Elysées, thousands cheered the Little General as he bowed left and right. The carriage and ponies were taken along as part of the theatrical equipment on all the troupe's trips through Europe and caused a sensation wherever Tom appeared.

The Barnum party next went to Spain, where Tom attended a bullfight with Queen Isabella, and then on to Belgium and further triumphs. The newspapers of the day reported that on their return trip to France, the Barnum carriages were held up in the mountains and Tom Thumb was kidnapped. The world waited breathlessly until Tom was found by shepherds in a cave. Since Barnum made no mention of this colorful episode in his memoirs, it was undoubtedly more of the famous Barnum "humbug," which paid off heavily at the box office.

Upon their return to America Barnum wrote that Tom's friends "found that he had not increased in size during the four and a half years of his absence but they discovered he had become sharp and witty, abounding in foreign airs and graces; in fact, that he was quite unlike the little, diffident country fellow they had formerly known. . . . He was an apt pupil, and I provided for him the best of teachers. . . . The General left America a diffident, uncultivated little boy; he came back an educated, accomplished little man. . . . He went abroad poor, and he came home rich."

Tom's father spent $30,000 of Tom's earnings on a large and impressive house in Bridgeport, putting into it a suite of rooms filled with exquisite miniature rosewood and mahogany furniture, much of which Mr. Stratton himself made. In a curio cabinet were displayed Tom's jeweled gifts of royalty — a Tom-size gold snuffbox set with turquoises, a tiny gold watch from Queen Adelaide, a ruby brooch from Queen Victoria, and an emerald and diamond stickpin from Louis Philippe. In the stables stood horses, ponies, and the carriages made for Tom in England. It was the first home the child had known since he left Bridgeport almost five years before, but he was soon put back on exhibit, accompanied by a tutor, while his family remained at home. He spent the next several years either at the museum in New York or touring here and in Europe.

In 1862, when the General met Lavinia Warren, his future wife, he was living in Bridgeport, making few public appearances, and enjoying his yacht and ponies. He was an active member of the Masonic Order, a wealthy man with extensive real estate holdings, and well able to retire on his vast earnings. Upon their marriage, Barnum generously released Mrs. Thumb from her contract, and following a wedding tour that included a visit with the Lincolns at the White House, the bride and groom retired to private life at the Stratton house in Bridgeport with Tom's mother (his father had died several years earlier). Perhaps there was a personality clash, but soon the General and Lavinia built a house in Middleborough, Massachusetts, opposite her mother's house, though they never really settled down.

Barnum notes in his recollections, "The General and his wife had been accustomed to excitement, and after a few months retirement they again longed for the peculiar pleasures of a public life. . . . They . . . have since travelled several years in Europe and considerably in this country, holding public exhibitions more than half the time, and spending the residue in leisurely viewing such cities . . . as they may happen to be in."

In addition to this restlessness, Tom developed a flagrant recklessness with money. According to Barnum, Tom Thumb, was miserly, as a child, but at maturity he became a profligate spender, wasting thousands on houses, jewels, horses, carriages, and yachts. When, on July 15, 1883, he died suddenly of apoplexy at his summer house in Wareham, Massachusetts, he left a very small estate to his widow. He was buried with full Masonic honors at Bridgeport, Connecticut.

What of Tom Thumb as a personality? There is no doubt that he was an enchanting child; he charmed Queen Victoria into three visits, the great Duke of Wellington repeatedly called on him and befriended him, and Louis Philippe invited him to the royal birthday celebration as a guest. It is interesting to note how little of the General's personality as an adult comes through in Barnum's writings, yet we get a distinct picture of Tom Thumb the child—a blithe, outgoing, unaffected little boy. Although the following is quoted out of context, which is always unfair, it seems to sum up not only what Barnum felt for Tom Thumb but what Tom Thumb the man felt about himself as others regarded him: "That is my piece of goods." Barnum's memoirs recount the strain put on the Little General as a child:

Besides giving daily entertainments, the General appeared occasionally for an hour, during the intermissions, at some place in the suburbs; and for a long time he appeared every day at the Zoological Gardens ... and when the General had gone through his performances on the little stage ... he was put into a balloon which ... was then passed around the ground just above the people's heads. ... One day, a sudden gust of wind took the balloon out of the hands of half the men ... and had not an alarm been instantly given ... the little General would have been lost. In addition to other engagements, the General frequently performed in the play, Hop O' My Thumb.

Still, compared to the children of that unenlightened day before child labor reforms, when children worked in mills or did piecework in dank cellars, little Tom Thumb was in many respects fortunate.

In *Barnum* (Harcourt Brace, 1923), Morris Robert Werner says of Tom Thumb in maturity, "He was very much a man of the world as soon as he was old enough to think. It was his body that he sold to the public, and it was his body that he always comforted; it is doubtful if he had much of a soul."

DIANNE L. SAMMARCO
AND KATHLEEN L. ROUNDS

■

The Seven Sutherland Sisters' Niagara of Curls

IN 1882 THE BARNUM AND BAILEY CIRCUS signed a new act for the sideshow. It was called the Seven Sutherland Sisters. The girls — Sarah, Victoria, Isabella, Grace, Naomi, Mary, and Dora, ranging in age from 18 to 36 — would file onstage in white gowns, their dark hair glimmering in the gaslights, and sing a selection of songs. The remarkable bass voice of Naomi was prominent in their rich harmony.

The music was not the chief attraction. The climax of the act came at the finale, when the sisters would turn in unison, letting their voluminous tresses — a collective total of 36½ feet of hair — spill down their backs, over the crest of the stage, and into the orchestra pit. A gasp of amazement and delight would sound through the audience, followed by thunderous applause. The act was a hit, but it was only the start of the saga of the Sutherland Sisters, a story more bizarre than any fiction writer could imagine.

The Sutherland girls were the offspring of a ne'er-do-well Vermonter, Fletcher Sutherland, and his wife, Mary, a student of music. Two of the daughters are listed on census records as adopted, and local speculation held that they were born to Martha Brink, Mary's sister, who lived in the Sutherland house. Martha cared for the Sutherland children after her sister died in 1867.

Raised in poverty and shunned by local society, the Sutherland sisters shared two assets — musical talent and rich, thick hair, which was said to be enhanced in its length and beauty by the use of a foul-smelling ointment brewed by their mother. Their musical abilities were what led Fletcher Sutherland to introduce his daughters to the world of the circus, but it was their hair that would make them rich. Naomi married J. Henry Bailey, nephew of the co-owner of the circus, in 1885. Bailey, knowing there were more bald men than music lovers, took over the management of the sisters' act. He started selling hair ointment, which Fletcher concocted from his late wife's formula, using the the Sutherland Sisters as his promotional tools.

The Seven Sutherland Sisters' Hair Grower and its related products — scalp cleaners, antidandruff potions, and hair coloring — made millions, thanks to the grueling promotional tours featuring a "Niagara of Curls." The sisters were able to build an ornate Victorian mansion on the site of their grandfather's log cabin in western New York state and supply each of the seven bedrooms with running water in marble bathrooms. To ensure a ready supply of water, a huge tank installed on top of the mansion was filled daily by workmen.

The money, which also flowed in like water, seemed to amplify the family's eccentricities. Pets were treated like royalty, with winter and summer wardrobes, grand funerals, and obituaries in the local newspapers. The carriage horses were shod in gold. The sisters sponsored many a gala event for the neighbors, often including fireworks.

All that money in the hands of a group of single women attracted adventurers. One of these was Frederick Castlemaine, who was thought to be sweet on Dora but who surprised everyone by marrying her older sister Isabella. He was 27; she was 40.

Castlemaine was handsome and charming but had a few eccentricities of his own, such as addictions to opium and morphine and the unnerving hobby of shooting the spokes out of wagon wheels from his seat on the Sutherlands' front porch. Impressive though his markmanship may have been, local farmers were unhappy about this practice. He salved their indignation with handsome payments. In 1897, while accompanying the sisters on one of their tours, Castlemaine committed suicide.

Tragedies such as this and the earlier death of one of the sisters,

Naomi, seemed to unhinge the remaining women. Naomi's body lay in state at the mansion for a number of weeks while construction of a $30,000 mausoleum was planned. But the plans were eventually abandoned, and Naomi was buried in the family plot without so much as a headstone.

When Fredrick died, the sisters brought his body home, and it, too, lay in state in the music room for several weeks, unembalmed, in a glass-domed casket. The sisters would visit the remains and sing Fredrick's favorite songs. Finally, the local health department intervened and forced the sisters to move the body to a $10,000 granite mausoleum. Even than, Isabella would walk the three miles to the cemetery every night, carrying a lantern, to commune with her late husband. This went on for two years, until she met and married Alonzo Swain. She was 46, and he was 30.

Swain persuaded Isabella to sell her shares in the family corporation and join him in an ill-fated attempt to sell a competing hair restorer whose formula called for nine quarts of English rum and two quarts of alcohol. The venture failed, Isabella died a pauper, and Alonzo disappeared.

Isabella's experiences with Castlemaine and Swain did not prevent Victoria Sutherland from marrying a 19-year-old man when she was 50. This caused a rift in the family, and the other sisters, who never married, refused to visit Victoria until she was on her deathbed.

The remaining women were dogged by other forms of misfortune. Mary had periods of insanity and was often kept locked in her room. The popularity of shorter hairstyles for women ended the success of the hair grower, and the fortune it had made for the sisters withered away. In 1926 the three surviving sisters went to Hollywood to help a studio make a movie about their lives, but the project was scrapped and Dora was killed in an auto accident there. She was cremated, but Mary and Grace had no money to pay for the services, so Dora's ashes remained in Hollywood.

The last two sisters returned to their decaying mansion and lived in the same poverty that had scarred the beginning of their lives. Eventually the house was sold. A few years after the death of the final surviving sister, the mansion burned to the ground, leaving only Castlemaine's grandiose mausoleum and, perhaps, a few dusty bottles of the Seven Sutherland Sisters' Hair Grower in attics and cellars to tell their story.

DON MUNSON

██████

The Amazing
Zerah Colburn

ZERAH COLBURN WAS BORN more than a century and a half ago in
Cabot, a small, remote hamlet in Vermont. By the time he was
eight years old, he was famous. At an age when most boys were happily playing marbles, Zerah was dazzling the scientists of two conti-
nents with his mathematical genius.

This strange and wonderful boy, born in 1804, possessed one of
the most remarkable brains of all time. He glanced briefly at
mathematics and knew all about it. Rumors spread all over Cale-
donia County about Abiah Colburn's boy's magical powers, and the
country folk gathered to witness them.

"How much is thirteen times ninty-seven?" one of the men
asked, no doubt passing a wink around the circle of skeptics.

"One thousand two hundred and sixty-one," the child replied
instantly. He was only six years old at the time.

Following a hasty conference and much computing, the elders
decided the answer was correct. "Wal, I swan!" they chorused, finding this phenomenon difficult to believe but impossible to deny.
Then they went to work to cook up even more difficult problems
for the eager child — to whom it was all play.

Zerah's father was a joiner, similar to what we now call a cabinetmaker, and it was while he was at work at his bench that the
strange story had its beginning. Zerah, playing in the chips on the
workshop floor, broke into a kind of chant: "Five times seven is
thirty-five; six times eight is forty-eight."

Colburn dropped his tools in astonishment. The child, after all,

69

was only six and had not been to school at all except for a few weeks during the previous summer. Second thought suggested that perhaps only a few multiplications had happened to stick in his mind. Not at all! He had more mathematical answers than his father had questions. A neighbor who had dropped in during the revelation left the house spraying news bulletins right and left. This is what brought on the inquisitors.

Abiah Colburn, who had waged a bitter struggle to make a living between his joiner's bench and his farm, now saw the family's horizons broadening. If little Zerah was one of the wonders of the world, as the sages of Cabot agreed, there should be a fortune in it.

That, of course, meant leaving Cabot. First stop Danville, the county seat, where members of the court questioned the boy; then to Montpelier to give members of the state legislature the same opportunity; to Burlington; Hanover, New Hampshire; and, at last, Boston, popularly described as the "Athens of America." Here in the American Athens, a distinguished panel, including James Perkins, Daniel Sargent, Josiah Quincy, William Sullivan, and William S. Shaw, confronted the boy from Vermont.

"How many," one of the inquisitors demanded, indecently it would seem, "how many seconds in two thousand years?"

For just a fraction of a minute, according to witnesses, the boy's body "assumed certain contortions." Then the triumphant treble: "730,000 days, 17,520,000 hours, 1,051,200,000 minutes, 63,072,000,000 seconds." The elders checked the answer and confirmed Zerah's findings.

There followed a tour of most metropolitan centers of importance on the Eastern Seaboard: New York, Philadelphia, Washington, Fredericksburg, Richmond, Charleston, and Norfolk. Then to Europe, a stormy passage of 38 days under sail before facing the scrutiny of the intellectual and aristocratic elite of Great Britain. Promises of sponsored education and other fulfillment flickered brightly in England, but deeds were laggard in following the words. A shrewd Yankee assessment of this led the harassed father to take his son across the English Channel to France.

In one of the salons of Paris, two extraordinary Americans crossed paths: the Vermont boy and Washington Irving. The handsome and gifted Irving greeted the Colburns with delight, as did William H. Crawford, U.S. minister to the court of Louis XVIII, and other distinguished Americans sojourning on the Seine. Probably the most extraordinary conjunction was that with the famous mathematician La Place, who took a very serious interest in the boy and suggested to the king that he be accepted for study at the Lyceum. Louis was too busy to get around to the application.

Shortly, Napoleon returned to France for his "one hundred days." He was fully capable of admiring Zerah's mind, having one of equal complexity, and managed to find time away from fighting off all of Europe to favor the boy with a scholarship at the Lyceum Napoleon. Other than the distinguished associations and the scholarship, Zerah's visit to Paris showed little profit. Perhaps the French were so dazzled by Napoleon's martial exploits that they had little appetite left for astonishment.

There were still friends in England, and the Colburns gave it another try. Thanks to the generosity of the Earl of Bristol, Zerah received a scholarship at Westminster School and studied there for almost four years before returning to the States. When he sailed from Southampton, the few years of education in France and England were all he had to show for 10 years of alternating high hopes and crushing disappointments. The Parisians didn't warm up to his lightning calculation, most of them probably being convinced that the most important mathematical knowledge is that one and one make two. The British showed greater ardor, especially the Earl of Bristol, who continued as Zerah's patron after almost everyone else had fallen away.

Zerah sailed for home not only without the promised fortune (he had his passage and $50 in his pocket, thanks to the Earl of Bristol) but also without his father, who had succumbed to tuberculosis. The voyage marked a complete break in the career of this prodigy. So far as the records show, he never again displayed his mathematical wizardry before a crowded auditorium. Evidently people were channeling their interests in other directions, and Zerah was seeking a new avenue of accomplishment.

Since the age of six a wanderer, though a fabulous and feted one, Zerah, upon arrival in America, headed straight for Cabot, Vermont, where he found an aged woman who didn't recognize her long-lost son and six brothers and two sisters—all living in impoverished circumstances. Though the house was small and humble, Zerah was welcomed and for the first time in 15 years felt that he was home. He also was deeply concerned about the family's problems. How could he help?

He tried an academic career first at "an academy in Fairfield, State of New York, connected with Hamilton College." (In the little writing he did, his style is a peculiar mixture of terse flatness with circumlocution and general disorganization. He was exact chiefly in lightning calculation.) After only a few months he resigned from the academy and returned to Cabot, having found "his prospects there quite different from what he had anticipated." (He usually spoke of himself in the third person.) Nobody but Zerah should have been surprised. The difficulties of patiently drilling the young would certainly seem tedious after years of easily astonishing his elders.

Zerah decided, after all his adventures abroad and his disappointment in his first attempt at teaching, to try preaching.

In the spiritual area he encountered difficulties easily as serious as those that had discouraged him in the educational field. A mathematical mind is addicted to having everything exact, which involves keeping a firm grip on seeing things in the small. Religion, however, finds its exactitude mostly through seeing things in the large.

During this struggle to check out his faith as to its exactness, he joined the Congregational Church in Burlington, Vermont, and after further soulful computation withdrew and was received into the Methodist Church. For nine years Zerah was a Methodist preacher, serving seven different circuits in Vermont, meanwhile acquiring a wife and three daughters. One wonders whether the small-town preaching seemed dull to him after Boston, London, Dublin, and Paris and after the Earl of Bristol, La Place, and Napoleon.

After almost a decade on the preaching circuit, he went back to teaching, giving as the reason his increased family responsibilities. During the last five years of his amazing life, he served as professor of languages at Norwich University in Norwich, Vermont.

Somehow he didn't belong, never could belong, because he was so different from other people. Questions that would seem impossible to us, he answered with ease. "Us?" To put it that way makes him an outsider, doesn't it?

One question that Zerah Colburn was never able to answer was what to do with his life. He was born to mystery, lived with it, and returned to it.

KATHRYN GRIFFIN

███

I Have a Dream for You, Mother

The world turns softly
Not to spill its lakes and rivers
The water is held in its arms
And the sky is held in the water.
What is water
That pours silver,
And can hold the sky?

— Hilda Conkling, age five

"THIS IS THE ERA of the child," wrote author Louis Untermeyer in his 1920 review of Hilda Conkling's *Poems by a Little Girl.* He went on to cite other well-known child prodigies in both Europe and America, implying that an age's preoccupation with wunderkinder might in some way be responsible for this book of "gifted" poems by a 10-year-old child.

Hilda Conkling began "saying" her poems at the age of four, and her mother, Grace Hazard Conkling, a poet herself and professor of English at Smith College, wrote them down and sent a few off to Harriet Munroe, editor of Chicago's prestigious *Poetry* magazine. Their publication occasioned quite a sensation and much speculation in literary circles. A year later, when Mrs. Conkling was looking for someone to write a preface for a collection of Hilda's poems, she was turned down by more than fifty literary acquaintances who preferred not to be associated with a possible hoax. But poet Amy Lowell enthusiastically championed Hilda's cause and wrote a laudatory preface to *Poems by a Little Girl* that did much to allay suspicions that Hilda's poetry was written by someone else.

Both Untermeyer and Lowell suggested that the mystery of how a young child could write good poetry lay in her ability to plumb the subconscious. Lowell said, "The only possible explanation is that the poems are perfectly instinctive ... Hilda is subconscious, not self-conscious." Untermeyer said, "The answer, I believe, lies in the child's very immaturity. It is the emotional primitive, still free of superimposed patterns, drawing its substance directly from the unconscious." Both writers expressed apprehension for Hilda's future as a poet.

Hilda published one other book of poetry, *Shoes of the Wind*, at age 12, and then *Silverhorn*, a selection of poetry she had written when she was between ages 8 and 10. She published some poems in the *Ladies' Home Journal, Good Housekeeping*, and *The Christian Science Monitor* when in her twenties. Her books were all long out of print by the time of her 71st birthday. It had been 61 years since her first book was published. She took the occasion to reminisce.

"'In Reverse' would be a good title for my autobiography," she said. "Some people struggle along and achieve the bestseller list in the forties and fifties. My forties and fifties came when I was ten. As the poetry shows, I found myself at age three or four.

"People say that my full potential hasn't been reached. But how does one know? Smith College tested me right, left, up, and down. It was discovered that I have a terrifying I.Q. of 186. I never remember learning to read—I was reading before I could speak clearly. Mother believed in intellectual stimulation at an early age and read poetry to my sister, Elsa, and me every night. Being a single parent—my mother and father were divorced when I was seven—she concentrated her whole attention on us. Mother disliked the word prodigy. Precocity, let's say.

"I talked poetry day and night, I guess. In any case, that was how *Poems by a Little Girl* came to appear. If it hadn't been for Harriet Munroe's publishing 'Songnets,' I might have been mumbling to myself forevermore and never been published at all.

"Only Amy Lowell would write the preface to my first book. People were taking sides that I couldn't have said such things, that my mother must have been writing through me. My mother was a close friend of Amy Lowell's for more than ten years, often visiting her weekends in Cambridge. They would stay up all night talking poetry. By writing the preface to *Poems by a Little Girl,* she launched my debut. I've always been grateful. She was a remarkable woman and poet. In the preface she said, 'What this book chiefly shows is high promise; but it also has its pages of real achievement, and that of so high an order it may well set us pondering.' She also said to my mother, 'If Hilda can survive the cutting-and-drying process of education, she will be a poet.'

"For me to describe the beginning is all hearsay, since I have forgotten the events leading up to the telling of my poems to Mother. All of this started when I was about four years old. My mother lectured widely on her own poetry as well as telling about me. One might say I came into a writing world and it was catching!

"I was born with a love of words plus a vivid imagination. My memory was later discovered to be photographic. Since Mother was always writing something in a notebook, I paid no attention to her scribbling during our conversations. It didn't register that she was taking down what I said, since I was busy in my own world. Even now it is difficult to explain what I was doing. I was conscious of saying things without understanding. That's about as close as you can come to inspiration. Mother recognized my free verse as something extraordinary."

> The river waits for water
> From a feeding stream;
> The little stream, winding,
> Runs on its way to pour itself
> Into the dying river
> And the river lives again
> In the valley.
> (Age 10)

"I have no feeling of ownership or identity with the poems — or of accomplishment — because I was like a clean blackboard, recording impressions. I think that any sensitive child might have these perceptions before they are squashed flat by parents' indifference or by school. To think they are mine, to think my mind produced them, astonishes me still. What I have done since can't compare. Most of my material ends up on the backs of envelopes destined to yellow with age. Not many have been published. I've written two novels and three children's stories, none of them published. I've been too busy earning a living.

"To become famous when one is small is hard on family and

friends as well as on oneself. Mother and my sister, Elsa, helped protect me from the curious and gushing souls swarming around asking for autographs. People behaved toward me not quite as if I were something out of the zoo, from another world, but certainly not human. One lady came and asked, 'How do you write a sonnet?" With aplomb, never having written a sonnet, I said politely, 'I don't know. You'll have to ask my mother about that.' She was my source of information and defense. When the first book appeared. Mother was determined that I think nothing remarkable had been done so that I would not think of myself as special or become conceited.

"In a way I wish I had been older to appreciate all the famous people who visited—Robert Frost, Vachel Lindsay, Walter De la Mare, and Carl Sandburg. I do remember walking along between Mother and Vachel Lindsay after one of his lectures. He was a man ahead of his time, a wonderful lecturer. He nearly took the roof off with his foot-stomping poem 'The Congo.' Mother must have asked him what would become of me. I can still hear him say over my head, 'God only knows, Grace. God only knows.' This seemed to be the only answer at the time."

> I have a dream for you, Mother,
> Like a soft thick fringe to hide your eyes.
> I have a surprise for you, Mother,
> Shaped like a strange butterfly.
> I have found a way of thinking
> To make you happy;
> I have made a song and a poem
> All twisted into one.
> If I sing, you listen;
> If I think, you know.
>
> From "For You, Mother,"
> dedication poem from
> *Poems by a Little Girl*

"My mother, after being trained abroad in the organ, transferred her talent to the piano. She'd practice eight hours a day trying to meet her highly critical standards. Nervous exhaustion eventually forced her to quit.

"Every time my mother played the piano I would sit dissolved in tears because all I could think of was that there would be a time when I wouldn't hear her play. I can still see myself to this day crying quietly in the dark while Mother played Chopin. I was seven or eight at the time.

"As I got older and more involved in school, the routine changed. It was get your homework done, do this and the other thing. I always disliked school, thought it a waste of time. I was a C student, barely passing most everything. Looking back, I think my problems in school were due to a combination of factors. The method of teaching then discouraged creative thinking, and anyone who was different, as I was, was apt to be ridiculed by schoolmates. With my photographic memory, I had difficulties with conceptual thinking. I had to be tutored in math, shown math concepts in a concrete way — five oranges plus four oranges equals nine oranges — before I could grasp it. While I ran the house and did the cooking, Mother would shut herself away in the afternoon quite busy with her college work. I tried to continue writing but found the act of writing things down hindered me. That's always been a hitch. The concept of a mental image and what turns up on paper suffers some change in the transfer. I don't know what happens, but it doesn't come out the way you think at all. Almost like a learning disability. It was a real handicap.

"Whenever I'd ask Mother for help or information, I was brushed off with, 'Never ask my help with your poems unless you feel sure it is the best you can do and are really stuck.' She meant to encourage self-discipline. With that encouragement I struggled by myself to complete a novel. I was trained never to interrupt her, although she was free to call me. Again and again I would reach out only to be thrown back on myself. Self-reliance became one of the first things I learned. "If Mother had continued listening to me after the first two books, I would have produced more. She squashed it by her routine.

"Mother-daughter relationships are quite something. The more I talk about myself and Mother, the clearer it comes in my mind. She was a very secretive, complex soul. More so than most. I admired her greatly and was her companion until her death. She died quietly in November 1958. If she had lived five more years, we might have become even better friends.

"Well-meaning folks often would ask, 'What do you want to be?' I didn't want to be anything. Never cared much for work. Born lazy, I guess. Mother couldn't believe she could have such a daughter. But as long as there were three meals on the table, I was perfectly content to stay at home and go on my own gentle way, not bothering anybody. Of course that couldn't go on indefinitely. Sometime I had to come out of my dreamworld and see what was going on.

"Until I was eighteen or twenty, Mother made decisions for me. She had to push me out of the house to get some training. All the time I would wonder — why go into the world to work? Through a friend of hers Mother got me a position at the South End House working with teenagers. I was so homesick on the train to Boston that I wanted to get right off and trot home again. From there it was on to a training school for kindergarten teachers. I could have stayed with that and been more sensible. But then I branched out in the bookstore business for over twenty years before taking on housekeeping for private families. Looking back at my life I see a series of chapters mostly paved with what might have been. If I were ever to come back, I would like to be an office assistant.

"Trepidation and lack of confidence have prevented me from sending out any more poetry. I've learned not to be overconfident, not to count on anything. I just rather shudder about sending the poems out and getting rejection slips. When a poem sells, it's to my utter surprise.

"So you might say that as one has a handicap from polio, I grew up with a handicap in regard to reality. While I was just trying to be an everyday child, this poetry intervened. It's like talking about another person, another life entirely. The thing that keeps me going is the expectation of the unexpected.

"In Cambridge in 1973, while I was working as a housekeeper, a man broke in through the dining room window. I woke up to find this strange kid in my room, about to attack me. When anyone grabs you by the neck, your hands come up automatically. He said, 'Put your hands down.' I obediently complied. I did not fight. He hit my nose three times. I was lying back with bare feet hanging out. He stepped back to admire his handiwork, and the oxygen got back into my brain. Boom! I swung my bare feet around and hit him just as low as I possibly could. I knocked him back against the closet door. He cracked his nose on the edge. Grabbing his nose, he went rushing down the stairs. When it was written up in the newspapers, they said the upstairs maid had four hundred dollars. I had four dollars in my purse. It took a long time to recover from two beautiful black eyes, but there was the satisfaction that I at last fought back.

"Looking back over it all, I think that I was something of a victim of my early success. My mother played the poetry down, as if it were nothing, played it down perhaps too much. She was over-protective and held me back in many ways. Twenty years of my life were put in parentheses. Dealing with a child prodigy, or gifted child as they say now, is complicated. Gifted children should be allowed plenty of time to themselves, to be thrown back on their own resources — time to read and think and imagine. They should not be made to mingle, be sociable, just because that's what is ex-pected of children. Parents should be nurturing, show interest, and provide stimulation as my mother did, but a child must be allowed to be himself or herself.

"I was my mother's daughter for too many years; she had a good strong temper, and sometimes when I was growing up, I was terri-fied of her. I would do almost anything to avoid a scene. Once when I was twenty-six or so, I was working on a poem but had not finished it and left it under a magazine when I went to bed. In the morning when I came down, Mother had found the poem and finished it. Well, I could have blown my top, but I just said, 'Let's send it to the *Monitor* and split the payment if they publish it.' I made $7.50.

"Probably I've been an actress all my life, playing the roles expected of me. Now I intend to play my own."

███

Heyday for Mellie

FOR SIX MONTHS from December 1925 through May 1926 Alanson Mellen Dunham, Jr., age 72, had more newspaper and magazine space devoted to him than did any other American in that same period. During the previous 71 years, "Mellie" Dunham had lived quietly on the 100-acre family farm on Crockett Ridge in Norway, Maine, doing the daily chores, making snowshoes, "huntin' and fishin'," and playing a mean fiddle for the area dances. There was little to indicate that Mellie, a sturdy, white-haired man with a flowing white mustache, would soon become a household word throughout the country.

He and his village schoolmate Emma were married in 1875, and their only child, Ethna Pearl, died giving birth to her ninth child. Following this, Mellie and Emma devoted themselves to helping their son-in-law, Nathan Noble, rear the nine grandchildren.

Before his meteoric rise to fame in late 1925, Mellie was known locally for his skill in making snowshoes. He started the snowshoe industry for which the town of Norway was subsequently famous. The quality of his workmanship and materials brought orders in about as fast as he could handle them. His son-in-law also became skilled in the profession.

The quality of Mellie's snowshoes attracted the attention of Commodore Robert Peary, the Arctic explorer, who visited Norway. Mellie designed a "Peary model" using the famous diamond weave, a pattern handed down to him by an old settler in the region, which eventually gained universal acceptance. Peary ordered 60 pairs for his famous trek to the North Pole in 1909. Peary's snowshoes can be seen today at the Smithsonian Institution.

For more than fifty years Mellie played the fiddle locally — and then the unbelievable happened. Reading about an old-time fiddlers' contest to be held at the Armory in Lewiston, Maine, in the fall of 1925, Mellie decided to enter just for the fun of it. He was probably a better snowshoe maker than fiddler, but he entered anyway. His son-in-law said, "Steer hide or fiddler string, he wasn't satisfied 'til he had got the best out of it."

Regardless of what it was that did it, on the eve of Mellie and Gram's golden wedding anniversary there was no stopping him. He swayed the huge crowd of seven thousand people in the Lewiston Armory with his magic bow and walked off amid thunderous applause with the championship cup as the best old-time fiddler in the state of Maine. And that would have been that, perhaps, except for a few sharp newspaper reporters. "Os" Brown, a Norway native working for a Boston newspaper, read about Mellie's winning the Maine championship, and he also read an item about some old-time fiddlers being invited to play for Henry Ford in Dearborn, Michigan.

The 1920s were jazz-crazy times, but Ford, the multimillionaire automobile magnate, did not like jazz. Because Ford found the dances of the jazz era immoral, he invested considerable money in an attempt "to revive square dancing, old-time kitchen dances, the hoe-downs, and to put on record the old native jigs and reels." This was all the incentive Os Brown needed. He showed the two articles to a Boston editor, contacted his friend Fred Sanborn, publisher of the weekly Norway paper, and then mailed the clipping about Mellie along with a letter to Ford. The wheels were in motion and would not stop until one of the most fantastic publicity stunts of all time carried Mellie Dunham into the national limelight.

In a couple of weeks Mellie received an invitation to visit Henry Ford in Dearborn and strut his stuff for the Michigan elite. There was nothing strange about such an invitation, as 38 other old-time fiddlers had already visited Dearborn at Ford's request, "performed a simple demonstration of the use of the resined bow," and returned home quietly. But none of them was from Maine, and none could compare with the picturesque figure and the dynamic natural showmanship of Mellie Dunham. This five-foot four-inch ball of fire, who "looked like a hammered-down Mark Twain" with his stocky frame, white hair and mustache, and "general Santa Claus appearance," offered too much for the public and the news media to let slide by.

In reply to Ford's first letter Mellie wrote, "I'll come as soon as

I can. I live on a farm, and you know we farmers must get ready for winter." He had to split wood, butcher animals, and get the supplies set up for the cold months ahead. When asked what he thought about the invitation, Mellie replied, "I can't imagine why Ford wants me. Perhaps it's because he never heard me play. Emma and I are ready for the time of our wild and wooly lives."

The day decided upon for the departure to Michigan was December 7, 1925, and a spectacular send-off was prepared by the Dunhams' neighbors, the village folks, and Os Brown. Emma Dunham was affectionately tagged "Gram" by the big-city reporters, photographers, and newsreel cameramen who descended on Norway for the send-off. Schools, shops, and mills were closed for the day, and a huge crowd gathered at the little Grand Trunk railroad station to lend their support.

The couple from Maine traveled to Montreal, where Mellie attended a banquet held in his honor by the Canadian Snowshoe Club. They arrived in Detroit the following day and in the next few days toured the Ford plant, played privately for Henry Ford, practiced with his orchestra for a private dance Ford had planned for 50 selected couples, and then played for the big dance itself on December 11, 1925, at the dance hall in the Ford engineering laboratory at Dearborn.

Mellie played many of his favorite tunes that night, including "Turkey in the Straw," "Portland Fancy," "Chorus Jig," "Old Zip Coon," "Arkansas Traveler," "Pop Goes the Weasel," and his most popular number, the "Rippling Waves Waltz," composed by none other than Mellie himself. Ford asked Gram to dance with him while Mellie played this famous composition and announced at the evening's end that he would keep Mellie and Gram there in Dearborn until his orchestra could learn the "Rippling Waves Waltz."

The shindig in Dearborn was mild compared to what was next in store for Mellie and Gram. After about two weeks in Dearborn, their pictures had appeared all over the nation in every major newspaper as well as in the movie newsreels. Another unbelievable opportunity arose — a chance to earn enough money to take good care of their grandchildren and ensure their education. Although they really missed Norway, and especially those nine kids, Mellie signed a contract to appear onstage with the Keith-Albee Vaudeville Circuit. It was too good to pass up. As a farmer and snowshoe maker, he had never made more than $20 in profits in a single week. Now he could earn $500 a week for 22 weeks from Keith-Albee, plus $100 a night for 50 nightclub appearances and an additional $3,200 from the Victor recording people for two records of his lively tunes. Not only would he earn around $20,000 himself, but he also would bring Norway and the state of Maine about $1 million worth of free publicity.

Mellie and Gram performed in 19 cities during those 22 weeks with a schedule that would have worn down a teenager. Their show took them to Boston, New York City, Philadelphia, Pittsburgh, Newark, Brooklyn, Providence, Baltimore, Washington, D. C., Cleveland, Detroit, Indianapolis, Cincinnati, Youngstown, Grand Rapids, Toledo, Syracuse, Lowell, Portland, and finally home again to Crockett Ridge in Norway. Asked about the hectic pace and how he was holding up under the strain, Mellie quipped, "They seem to be afraid I won't last out the trip. They don't know the stuff the old people of Maine are made of."

The Dunhams met many important people during their whirlwind tour. The governor of Massachusetts welcomed them to the Bay State, and Mellie received a key to the city of Boston. In New York City he was greeted at city hall, and the stock exchange on Wall Street closed a few minutes early to host a visit from the Norway nomad. Dignitaries in other states also welcomed the affable couple from Maine, but the biggest event occurred in Washington, D.C. On Monday, March 1, 1926, the first day of their arrival in the capital city, Mellie and Gram called on President Coolidge at the White House, where they were warmly received.

In Cleveland Mellie's name blazed on an electric sign over the street, and there were eight-foot-high pictures of him on both sides of the theater entrance. In Indianapolis, where Mellie and Gram had a suite of rooms with a kitchen at the Spink Arms Hotel, Mellie wrote home, "One act on our bill has a lot of fowls in it — turkeys, hens, geese, etc. One of the geese laid an egg yesterday and they gave it to Emma. We had it for our breakfast."

Obviously, Mellie and Gram were having a great time on the circuit, even though they did seem a little out of place in the strange big-city world. Nevertheless, they remained unaffected by all the stardom and were just themselves from beginning to end. The bright lights, applause, and news coverage meant just one thing to them. As Mellie told a Philadelphia reporter, "Back home are nine motherless grandchildren, and when the wife and I get back there we will be able to see them through. If I fill the engagement, I will have enough money for them, and if I fall dead on the threshold of my house the day I get back, I will still feel that this was the one act of my life and the best of all."

After 22 weeks on the road and almost 6 months away from home, Mellie and Gram returned to Norway on May 24, 1926. When the train drew in to the local station, thousands of people, young and old, let out a mighty cheer. Flags waved, bands played, the youngsters displayed their cardboard fiddles, and a big parade carried them to the platform constructed in the town square. On the speakers' stand Donald Partridge of Norway officially welcomed the famous couple back with true hospitality. "Though there have been similar demonstrations for Mellie and Gram," he said, "many have been of a purely curious nature. Here we are not curious. We know Mellie and Gram too well. We are just sincerely expressing our respect and love." After speaking of the many honors that had come Mellie's way, Partridge concluded by remarking, "Only three Americans are known to the world by their nicknames — 'Teddy' Roosevelt, 'Abe' Lincoln, and 'Mellie' Dunham."

This was a little too much for Mellie, but he was obviously tickled by the flattery. For the next 45 minutes he and Gram stood shaking hands with all their old friends as Company C of the 103rd Infantry guided people to the stand.

Now that the unbelievable had happened and come to an end, how did the 72-year-old Mellie feel about it all? "Any man has a chance in life as long as he lives. Six months ago I didn't have a hope in the world, and now I wouldn't swap places with the president."

Yet with all his happiness and optimism, Mellie realized the big time had come to an end, and he was a little sad. "Saturday night always comes. That's the only trouble with show business. I've made lots of friends in every city I've been in, and Saturday nights I have to leave them. Of course I'm mighty glad to get home, but I hate to leave so many nice folks. But then, that's the way of life. Saturday night always comes and you have to leave the friends you've made."

4

RISK TAKERS

RICHARD W. O'DONNELL

The Original Human Fly

THE CLIMBER HAD REACHED the 30th floor. He had only 27 more floors to go to reach the top. That memorable spring day in 1920, the man from Marblehead, Massachusetts, had inched his way, slowly but surely, up the outside of New York's famous Woolworth Building, which, at the time, was the highest building in the United States. In the street below, tens of thousands of New Yorkers, all of them nervous, stared up at the intrepid climber. Traffic was stalled for blocks around. The city was at a standstill. Would he make it all the way to the top, or wouldn't he?

When the daredevil reached the 30th floor, something happened, and his heroic climb came to an end. That brave climber did not fall — nothing like that. It was the long arm of the law that got in his way. When the chap reached the 30th floor, a police sergeant stuck his head out a window and asked, "Have you got a permit from the City of New York to do this?"

The man dangling on the outside of the skyscraper informed the law enforcement official that he had neglected to obtain a permit.

"Then, sir," said the sergeant solemnly, "I'll have to ask you to come inside. You've snarled traffic all over downtown New York. Nothing's moving. Everybody's in the street below looking up at you. I'm sorry, sir, but you are under arrest for climbing a building without a permit."

Thus did the great climb come to an end, and it was probably the most unusual arrest ever made by a New York police officer.

In his day George Gibson Polley, who died in 1927, climbed —by his own count—more than two thousand buildings in the United States. Never once did he slip or lose his grip. He was known as the "Original Human Fly," and his building-climbing accomplishments stagger the imagination.

In Boston he climbed up the side of the Custom House and the Little Building. In Lynn he climbed the old city hall. He also climbed the city hall in Portland, Maine. In Manchester, New Hampshire, he went all the way up the side of the tallest hotel in town. Over in Vermont the "Tarzan of the Cities," as he was being billed, climbed up the side of a Montpelier department store. The building was only four floors high, but it was the tallest thing Polley could find in town. In Hartford, Connecticut, Polley climbed up the side of three buildings in one day. And over in Providence, Rhode Island, for a change of pace, he put on a blindfold and climbed all the way to the top of the tallest flagpole in town. Polley climbed the old Cregg Building at Common and Amesbury streets in Lawrence, Massachusetts, so many times that he could go up the side of that structure wearing a blindfold, too.

"My father was a daredevil, but he never took any unnecessary chances," recalled his son, G. Gibson Polley, a realtor in Marblehead and Hamilton, Massachusetts. "Before he went up the side of a building, he always checked out the exterior to make sure there were no loose bricks or that the wood hadn't rotted away. He used to grab drainpipes as he was going up, and if they were weak, he would not risk a climb. If he considered the outside of a building dangerous, he'd find another one in the same town. Or, if necessary, he'd cancel his climb.

"He used to say he was 'a daredevil and not a fool.' And before he started up the side of a building, he would make a short speech warning youngsters not to try what he was going to do. He made it clear to the youngsters that it took a great deal of training to do what he did. My father didn't drink or smoke or even swear. He always kept himself in top physical condition. He was quite a man.

Actually, George Polley's career as a human fly started when he was a mere lad in Richmond, Virginia, where he was born. He loved to play baseball, and one day during a sandlot game he hit a home run. The only baseball available ended up on the roof of a six-story school building. So George climbed up the side of the structure and recovered the ball.

In 1910, when he was 12, George's family moved to Chicago, and he got a job delivering newspapers. One afternoon, after delivering a paper to a well-known Chicago clothing store, he spotted an expensive suit hanging on the rack. "Boy," he told the store owner, "I'd stand on my head on the top of this building if I could have a suit like that."

Naturally, the clothing store owner thought the lad was joking. "If you do that," he said with a friendly smile, "I'll be glad to give you the suit."

So young Polley went outside, took off his coat, climbed to the top of the three-story building, and stood on his head. And the newsboy had a new suit. In later years he sometimes wore a sign on his back naming the product or organization he was publicizing.

Polley's climb up the side of the clothing store attracted a great deal of attention, and he was offered a contract by a local theater manager. Thus was his fantastic career launched. The great Houdini taught the youngster some tricks of magic, and at the age of 13 he was billed as "The World's Youngest Magician" With Houdini's help, he also became an outstanding escape artist. But it was his daring as the "Original Human Fly" that brought Polley his greatest fame.

Much of his success was due to his flair for showmanship. His arrival in a town was treated as headline news by the local press. He invited reporters to join him when he inspected the building he was scheduled to climb, and he always announced that the particular building he was going to climb was "one of the most dangerous" he had come across.

He usually wore a white suit and sneakers as he went up the side of a building. And if he thought it could be done safely, he would deliberately "slip" and drop a floor to the ledge below at least once during a climb.

When World War I broke out, Polley joined the army and served in France as a sergeant in the Observation Balloon Corps. "After the war my father would never accept a penny when he performed for the American Legion or the Salvation Army," Gibson said. "He was a member of the Legion and was always willing to perform when they wanted to raise funds. He remembered how the Salvation Army kept serving coffee and donuts to the boys up front during the war, and he was willing to help the Salvation Army when that fine organization needed to raise money."

After the war Polley met and married the former Helen Stillman. His wife was a singer, and they appeared many times together on stage. After their marriage the couple settled in Helen's hometown of Marblehead. In addition to Gibson, they had two other sons; Herbert, who was killed in action with the army during the Second World War, and Stillman, a Miami businessman.

During the 1920s many so-called human flies crept up buildings in various parts of the nation. But Polley was the originator of the daredevil act and easily the most successful. He would climb buildings to attract crowds to his magic shows in local theaters. Or he would be hired by store owners to attract crowds to their grand openings or to lure people to carnivals sponsored by civic organizations.

His standard fee for climbing a building was $200. A Springfield, Massachusetts, newspaper used to hire him every December to climb a building in that city. While he was climbing, newsboys would circulate through the crowd below and collect funds to buy toys for the poor children of the community. It should be noted that Polley added his own salary to this particular collection.

"Human Fly" Polley was also an automobile salesman. In fact, he was probably the most successful salesman the old Essex car company every had. He would arrive in a town and inform the press that he was about to climb the tallest building available. The press would headline the news, and at the appointed time Polley would appear and climb the building. Then he would climb back down and start shaking hands with every person present. He also would hand a small card to each one he greeted, urging one and all to visit the local distributor of Essex motorcars. Finally, he would saunter over to his own magnificent new Essex, start up the engine, and head for the next town, where more potential customers were anxiously waiting for him to climb one of their buildings.

Besides standing on his head when he reached the roof of a building, Polley sometimes rode a bicycle around the edge of the roof. Actually, the wheels of the bike were in the drainpipe at the side of the building, which made the feat all the more sensational.

In scaling skyscrapers in practically every major city in the nation, he had his share of close shaves. Once, while going up a building in a southern community, it was necessary for him to grab two copper pipes. As he was raising his body, one of the pipes broke and struck him on the side of the head. Polley, though bleeding, managed to reach the top safely, but the wound required several stitches.

George Gibson Polley, who defied death practically every day of his adult life, passed away at the age of 29 during an operation for a brain tumor. He once told an interviewer, "I regard my vocation strictly as a business, and I assure you I am very glad when a climb is completed. I've climbed more than two thousand buildings during my career, and haven't fallen yet. And I don't expect to." He never did.

SCOTT CRAMER

The Big Catch

ON JULY 7, 1985, Paul Tavilla of Arlington, Massachusetts, caught a grape tossed from the top of the 38-story, 528-foot National Shawmut Bank Building in Boston, setting a new world record. He had it captured on videotape, "in slow motion. . . . You should see the grape splattering in my mouth!" He was then 50 years old, a part owner of P. Tavilla Produce Company.

Paul Tavilla discovered his ability to catch objects in his mouth as a boy. He amazed his brothers and sisters by catching cherry tomatoes, strawberries, small plums, grapes, and pieces of banana tossed short distances. Later he impressed army buddies who tossed him pieces of hot dogs.

Paul's talent went largely unheralded until 1977. In July of that year a friend sent him a newspaper clipping that reported the world record for catching a thrown grape in the mouth was 204 feet, set in 1974 by Arden Chapman of Louisiana. The friend wrote on the clipping, "Paul. I'll match you with the champ anytime." Two weeks later, after learning that Chapman had set a new world record of 243 feet, Paul caught a black California Ribier grape thrown 251 feet, which earned him a spot in the 1978 *Guinness Book of World Records*.

By the mid-1980's, the Louisianian had claimed to have caught a grape thrown 319 feet. Paul didn't believe a grape could be thrown that far and offered the person who allegedly threw the grape $10,000 plus an all-expense-paid trip to Boston to do it again. He had no response. If his 1985 record were to be broken, Paul said he would attempt to catch a grape tossed from Boston's John Hancock building, some 700 feet high.

Paul was often asked questions such as "What if the grape hits you in the eye?" "Can it go down your throat?" "How fast does the grape go?" To set the record straight, he agreed to discuss his big catch and even give a few pointers to those inclined to attempt the feat.

"Use the proper grape," he insisted in a 1985 interview. Because of its size, weight, color, and availability, Paul's grape of choice has been the black California Ribier. "I've tried other grapes," he said, "but I always return to the Ribier. They're the easiest to see." He once painted grapes Day-Glo orange; they were easy to see but hard to throw.

Skyscraper selection is just as important as grape selection. "A grape stands out best against a light-colored building," Paul said. "The building's height doesn't matter because you can't see the grape until it's halfway down anyway."

Getting permission to toss a grape from the rooftop of some buildings may be difficult. Before Paul was allowed to attempt his big catch, he had to sign a waiver that released the Shawmut Bank from legal damages in the event that a bystander got hit by a grape.

Paul always warmed up before attempting any big catch and suggested that others do the same. On the street he would stand 20 feet from a person who would throw him fastballs. "I find it helps me relax, lets me limber up. It gives me confidence."

From 1977 to 1985 Paul's thrower was Mike Weir, a police officer. When Mike developed arm trouble, Paul enlisted his coworker, John Barronshian, to toss the grapes off the building. The hour of the big catch, however, John was stuck in Cape Cod traffic, so Paul's friend from church, Paul Gannon, substituted. Paul gave him a bunch of grapes and instructed him to toss one every three seconds.

Paul stood one hundred feet from the building. "Grapes were landing on my left. Grapes were landing on my right. One hit the roof of a car. The sound it made was incredible, like a bullet. There was nothing left of it. Just juice."

Paul never feared speeding grapes, which he'd been told travel close to 100 miles per hour at impact. "Don't get me wrong. I could slip and have one hit me in the eye. But I'm not worried. I follow the grape with my eye and know how I'm standing. I'd never try it on a windy day."

He said it's highly unlikely that a grape could go down his throat. "When your head is tilted back, the grape lands in the bottom of your mouth."

Paul tried to catch only three grapes that day in Boston. "I was very selective. I went for the ones that looked like they would land right over my head. At the last second I cranked my head back.

"The first one hit me on the lip and gave me a fat lip. The second one hit my chest. It stung pretty good. But I got the third one." Paul laughed. "The one I got turned out to be the last grape of the bunch."

JOHN J. GALLIVAN

Scalped
by General Fremont

THE MORNING SUN streaming into the office of the Barnum Museum in the late spring of 1860 fell upon two men engaged in earnest conversation. A greater dissimilarity of appearance would be hard to visualize — the great P.T. himself, faultlessly attired and tonsorially correct, and the man seated opposite him resembling a creature from another world. His hair hung to his shoulders, and a great bush of beard covered most of his face and chest. Except for a deerskin cap decorated with fox tails and the greasy buckskins that constituted the balance of his costume, he might have stepped out of the Book of Prophets. Yet, in spite of the physical differences that would seem to set them poles apart, there was a meeting of minds, a solidarity of thought expressed in their talk, for both were superb showmen and both possessed a flair for the spectacular.

Barnum, was in the process of trying to recoup his fortune after a disastrous venture into the clock-making field. The Barnum Museum, which he had disposed of prior to what he had fondly supposed to be his retirement from show business, had been doing poorly. The new owners had learned, sadly, that all entrepreneurs are not necessarily showmen, even as Barnum had learned that all showmen are not necessarily clock makers. A change of ownership was effected, and once again Barnum was looking for new and unusual attractions to provide drawing power for his show.

The frontiersman seated opposite Barnum was the great "Grizzly" Adams, recently disembarked from the clipper ship *Golden Fleece* after a journey of three and one-half months "round the Horn" from California. Adams, had brought with him his collection of California animals that had formed the nucleus of his own museum in San Francisco, including a number of grizzly bears, the most notable of which was Sampson, who tipped the scale at more than three-quarters of a ton, the largest grizzly ever captured. Besides an assortment of lesser bears, he had buffalo, lions, elks, wolves, foxes, and Old Neptune, great sea lion of the Pacific. It was indeed a tremendous attraction that Barnum was dickering for, and the details were just now falling into place to the satisfaction of both.

After coming to what amounted to a fifty-fifty agreement, Adams removed the hat he wore both indoors and out and showed Barnum his head. "His skull was literally broken in," wrote Barnum in his memoirs. "It had on various occasions been struck by the fearful paws of his grizzly students; and the last blow, from the bear called 'General Fremont,' had opened his brain so that the workings were plainly visible!" Barnum wrote that the wound looked particularly dangerous and expressed the thought that it might prove fatal. Adams agreed, stating that he was a "used-up man" and, as though discussing an animal that was to be destroyed, that he doubted that he had six months to live. He had no intention of going off somewhere to lie down and await the end, however, and during the next six months, if that proved to be his time, he expected to provide a heap of living.

John Capen Adams had been born in Medway, Massachusetts, on October 22, 1812, one of the seventh generation of the illustrious Adams family that had at that time provided more than its quota of famous men, including two presidents. He was the son of Henry and Sybil (Capen) Adams of that small New England community and at an early age was apprenticed to the trade of shoemaking. However, he found little to his liking in shoes, as he was from early childhood a lover of the outdoors. After serving his apprenticeship, he became associated as a collector of wild animals with a group of men who were conducting circuses throughout the East. As a result of this connection, he trapped and captured alive most of the species native to New England at the time — foxes, wolves, wildcats, panthers, and deer — and tramped the wilderness from Maine through western Massachusetts. Hunting was entirely to his satisfaction, not so much as a means of livelihood as a way of life, and with Adams life seemed good.

Things might have continued along indefinitely in this idealistic outdoor existence except for the mean disposition of a Bengal tiger that was the pièce de résistance of the circus. The owners had imported the tiger at considerable expense, but it had become so recalcitrant that they finally called in Adams from the field to attempt to salvage their investment. The hunter, with the same quiet courage that was to mark many later encounters with even bigger and more savage beasts, entered the cage to deal with the tiger and was nearly killed. He hovered between life and death for weeks but finally recovered, although injuries to his spine left him a partial invalid. The hope of continuing the outdoor life that he loved was shattered. He was at a loss even as to a means of livelihood.

"Nothing," Adams philosophized, "is ever wasted, and my early training in the bootmaking field now prevented me from becoming a public charge." And for a matter of some 15 years the shoemaker stuck to his last, not only supporting himself but becoming a man of substance and a husband and father. About 1849 he attempted to better his situation by investing his accumulated savings of about $7,000 in a shipment of shoes to the Midwest. He went personally to St. Louis, arriving just in time to see his entire stock in trade destroyed in a warehouse fire. Wiped out, he had no heart to return to New England. He decided to go on to California, swept up by the dream of sudden wealth that ran like wildfire through the entire nation during the gold rush of '49.

Adams arrived in California in the fall of 1849, having traveled overland by way of Mexico. He embarked on one venture after another, trying in quick succession mining, farming, and ranching. In a period of a little over three years he made and lost several fortunes. He lost on defective mining claims, lost through crop failures, and lost a huge herd to rustlers while ranching. Finally, in disgust, he decided to withdraw from the world of man and retired to a lonely section of the high Sierras with the thought of becoming a hermit. His worldly goods consisted of a rugged wagon, a yoke of oxen, a Kentucky large-bore rifle, a Tennessee rifle of smaller bore, a Colt revolver, and a meager assortment of tools and clothing.

The mountains acted as a balm to the soul of John Adams. The clean air, sparkling mountain streams, evergreen forests, and plentiful supply of game soon made him forget the frowns of fortune and the raw dealing of his fellow men. Here was the carefree, rugged life of his hunting days returned. His strength and health were restored, and once again life was good. The man who had forsaken the haunts of men, disillusioned and wounded in spirit, was restored to the confident outdoorsman.

The winter passed in blissful solitude. With the coming of spring his brother William located him in his mountain fastness. William had enjoyed a considerable measure of success in the goldfields and wanted John to accompany him home to New England, even offering to set him up in business again. But John's pride stood like an invisible barrier between him and Massachusetts. Seeing how matters stood, William made a generous offer that molded the hunter's future into a pattern he could not resist. William offered to provide letters of credit for supplies and equipment if his brother would take up hunting again in earnest, with William acting as agent in the East to handle the sale and distribution of the animals captured. The deal was made and a partnership formed that was to work out very well for both.

For three years Adams hunted the mountain regions, ranging over the Rockies and the Sierra Nevada and traveling north into Oregon and Washington and out onto the plains as far as Utah. He camped in many wild spots, among Indians, miners, vaqueros, and bad men. Each year his collection grew, and each year he returned to winter in the high Sierras, in a little valley on the north branch of the Merced River, near Yosemite.

The first year Adams had not given the grizzly bears much thought and had certainly not earned the nickname by which he was to become universally known. In common with other hunters he usually gave the huge beasts a comfortably wide berth, for his small experience with them to date had led him to form the conviction that the huge beasts were second to none in courage, even including the African lion and the tiger of Asia. Eventually it was to reach a point where he considered it a matter of honor to do battle with the behemoths if he even got news of one being in the neighborhood. His first brush with them was to come shortly.

In the next valley the local Indians discovered an old female with two yearling cubs, evidently with a den close by. Grizzly determined to start his collection with two cubs. Lying in wait by the trail, he shot the mother. He then rushed forth and attempted to lasso one of the cubs. But a yearling grizzly is an animal to be reckoned with. The net result was a reversal of the hunt, with Adams dropping his rifle and climbing a tree to get away from the furious beast. He captured both cubs by chasing them for several miles on horseback. When they became weak from exhaustion, he readily lassoed them. And so Grizzly Adams had the start of a collection that was to become nationally and world famous. The female cub he named Lady Washington. She became his friend and faithful companion second only to one—the doughty Ben Franklin. In similar fashion he acquired several browns and cinnamons, until he had about eight young bears about the place and the problem of food became a major one.

The native antelope abounded in the region. Though they are among the sharpest-sighted and kneenest-scented of animals, Adams learned that they fell easy prey to their own curiosity. He found that by lying on the ground with his legs waving in the air or by fluttering a scrap of red cloth he could bring the inquisitive beasts flocking about.

The collection grew, and Adams continued to ship animals east for zoos and circuses, reserving a superior specimen here and there to form the nucleus of his own collection. Always the great grizzly had a peculiar fascination for him. He contended that it was the most intelligent and responsive of all animals.

The life a collector of animals was of necessity a rugged one. On many occasions he came to mortal combat at knife range with wolves, elks, and buffalo, as well as bears. He was pawed, chawed, charged, tossed, and trampled by every conceivable animal of the western plains and mountains. Either he possessed a charmed life or was a fool for luck. After three years there was still sufficient of him left in one piece to proceed to civilized California, where he opened museums in a number of towns and finally ended up with his Pacific Museum in San Francisco.

There a young newspaperman named Theodore H. Hittell came to frequent his establishment, first in search of items for the *Evening Bulletin* and finally as Grizzly's personal biographer. It was he who chronicled the capture of the great behemoths—Lady Washington, Ben Franklin, Jackson, General Fremont, and the rest. Hittell's book is a fascinating piece of writing from a standpoint of adventure, but from a biographical angle it contains a rather startling and entirely unfortunate error. He didn't quite catch the name! Adams's given name was John. Hittell thought it was James.

Depsite three successful years in San Francisco with his museum, in early 1860 Adams was almost as poor as the day he arrived in California in 1849, due to poor management and lack of business knowledge. It was at this point he decided to move to New

York in an attempt to recoup his fortune. The long journey around the Horn with his assortment of animals proved his undoing, for it was during the voyage that he received the terrible blow from General Fremont that was eventually to cause his death.

After contracting with Barnum he exhibited his beloved animals for as long as he could, but his health failed steadily. In early October he retired to his family home in Neponset, Massachusetts, where he died peacefully on October 25, 1860.

BOB TREBILCOCK

In Search of Sasquatch

AL DAVIS, A CUSTODIAN who lived in West Rutland, Vermont, called himself a "no-nonsense-type person," a man who would "never say I seen something unless I seen it. I don't want people laughing at me." Which is why he always hesitated to say what it was that he and members of his family saw on September 20, 1985, behind his house on Route 4A following his grandmother's funeral.

"I heard something *big* coming my way. The first thing I thought was that one of the neighbor's cows had gotten loose. I figured I'd better get out of the way and stepped off the trail. There was a valley-type wind that night, and this sickening smell came up through. When I saw this thing, I was petrified. It was like someone pulled back the hammer of a gun and pointed it at me. It was that kind of fear. I watched it for thirty yards or so. More or less what I saw was a silhouette under the streetlight there. It looked like a gorilla. It walked like a man, on two feet, had a distinct swaying motion of the shoulders, and had real long arms."

He'd seen bears, knew what they looked like, and this didn't look like that, he said. It was "something," he said, that "I don't ever want to see again."

Several days following the inexplicable encounter at the Davises', Dr. Warren Cook, then a 61-year-old professor of history and anthropology at Castleton (Vermont) State College, made plaster casts of the footprints. On his dinner table the casts looked like discarded displays from a shoe store for basketball players.

"I believe they're genuine," said Dr. Cook, one of only two academic scholars in the nation admitting to research on the subject. "Whatever made them, eight people heard it, seven people smelled it, and four people saw it."

That the legendary Sasquatch, also known as Bigfoot — a giant half-man, half-ape thought to be the evolutionary missing link — might roam rural New England came as no surprise to Warren Cook. These beasts had been spotted in all the New England states except Rhode Island. Over the previous 10 years, Dr. Cook had collected more than 140 references to Bigfoot in New England and the New York counties bordering Vermont, dating back to 1603 when Champlain recorded the Indian legend of Gaugou, a human-like beast believed to be a devil.

There had been more sightings in New England than anywhere else, with the exception of Florida and the Pacific Northwest. One gentleman from Windsor County, Vermont, was so shaken by the "animal-man" he saw along Highway 91 that he cried as he told his wife. A good many accounts recalled a haunting Sasquatch sound, as high-pitched and forlorn as a train whistle. One Vermont woman was reminded of the pain and loneliness of childbirth.

"My guess is he's more ape than man," Dr. Cook said. "Different versions of man intermingled. Sasquatch didn't. He went out on his own from the African plains and adapted to the cold and to swamps."

The general scientific attitude toward Bigfoot had long been at best wildly skeptical. Dr. Richard Thorington, a primate specialist at the National Museum of Natural History, said he thought Dr.

Cook was sincere but that "someone is having a fine time playing a prank on him."

One might wonder why Dr. Cook would have risked his credibility on a subject associated with tabloid headlines. "I'd rather investigate things that aren't understood than regurgitate on subjects already covered," he said. Every native tribe from the Eskimo to the Central American Indians, he pointed out, had a name for these creatures. It wasn't the legends that captured Dr. Cook's attention but the persistence of encounters through the ages. He was accustomed to the naysayers. "It's outside the mind-set," he explained. "If you go against the accepted paradigm, you have to prove your point."

Dr. Cook had a 35-mm slide, taken in the fall of 1977 by a photographer whose identity Dr. Cook wouldn't reveal, that depicted a wooded nature trail in northeastern Rutland County. In the center of the picture was a broad, dark object with two points of white where eyes might have been. When viewed in relation to other objects, the dark thing became formidable — maybe seven feet tall and broad. The slide came into Dr. Cook's possession through an acquaintance. He had it examined and found that it hadn't been tampered with.

"I couldn't really distinguish features," Dr. Cook explained. "So my theory was that it was an upturned stump." He visited the site. There was no evidence that anything large had been upturned from the soil. Dr. Cook concluded that something as big as the object in the photo wouldn't have deteriorated in just five years and a depression that big wouldn't have filled in.

"Whatever was in that photograph," he said, "is a thing capable of moving itself or readily being moved. That put a Bigfoot allegedly in the area." Dr. Cook subsequently interviewed a woman who had sighted something resembling an ape-man around the date the photograph had been taken. In nearby Washington County, New York, at least eight Bigfoot encounters had been recorded since 1976.

But a big question still remains: Why don't we find a body? Dr. Cook said that the beasts may have a sense of death and take care of the remains of their ancestors. But his most convincing argument might be that we rarely find the corpses of other large mammals that haven't been shot by man. "Quite simply," Dr. Cook said, "I think Sasquatches know more about our habits in their environment than we know about them."

The Crash Hunter

IT HAPPENED AT 6:10 P.M., April 17, 1944. Two Navy F6F-3 Hellcat fighter aircraft on a training mission collided over South Kingston, Rhode Island, and crashed several miles away in a dense cedar swamp, killing both pilots. Larry Webster, who researched the accident much later, learned that the planes had been based at the Charlestown Naval Air Station. On that fateful spring evening, he believed, they were flying in close formation at an altitude of 2,500 feet when one aircraft's left wingtip pushed into the other's cockpit and then its prop chewed up the other's right outer wing. The first plane began rotating and landed on its back in the swamp. The other crashed and partially burned 200 yards away. He believed the pilots may have been blinded by the setting sun.

Forty-four years later, in early March, Webster was tramping through the still-frozen swamp, picking his way among a thick profusion of vines, briers, branches, rhododendrons, cedars, and pines. It was hard going. "The mob could dump a body in here, and nobody would ever find it," he told a companion.

He had last been there nearly two decades earlier, when he located the wreckage of 9B. Larry kept files on the three hundred crashed military aircraft he'd located. Each file, a numbered, single sheet of paper, contained information on the pilot, weather conditions, cause and location of the crash, eyewitness reports, wreckage, remains, and "other particulars."

The file numbers for the two Hellcats that had collided over South Kingston were 9A and 9B. He located 9A, the plane that partially burned, in 1963. But he did not find 9B until 1969, and only then because of a bizarre set of circumstances. Until then the wreckage had remained undisturbed for 25 years. Now he had returned to show me the site.

"It's going to be embarrassing if I can't find it. This seemed so much easier when I was twenty years old," he said, breathing heavily. Larry, 39, had broad shoulders and a strong, compact body, but moving through the swamp was vigorous work.

He had three landmarks to find: a stone wall, a tall tree, and his own 19-year-old path. While southern Rhode Island had changed dramatically over the previous several decades, change occurs slowly in a swamp. It could take a century for a cedar to reach maximum height and centuries more for it to die. Drainage ditches and fire ponds dug by Civilian Conservation Corps (CCC) workers in the 1930s looked, as though they could have been dug a year ago. Larry, who had done a fair share of digging himself in the swamp, said the leaves were green three inches below the muck. Everything was preserved. He fully expected to find where he sawed off branches 19 years earlier.

Larry had lived in Charlestown, Rhode Island all his life. Military aircraft had always fascinated him. As a boy he saw planes passing overhead to and from the naval air stations at Charlestown and Quonset Point. Both bases, long since closed, served as training sites for pilots during and after World War II.

In 1962, when he was 15, his parents suggested that he try to find some of the local crash sites. "I must have been a pest that day. They wanted me out of the house." Since 1940 approximately fifty planes had crashed within a 10-mile radius of his home.

Several weeks later he and a cousin located the scattered remnants of a Hellcat that had crashed on Mother's Day 1944. "I felt as though I had gone back in time when I started finding pieces. It was a very strange sensation," he recalled. His cousin soon lost interest (as would many others who joined him on crash hunts over the years), but Larry spent the rest of the summer riding his bicycle to the site and probing the ground for pieces with a metal pole. He dug them up and carried them home in a bag — in all, 2,500 pounds. An entire Hellcat weighed 9,600 pounds.

His hauling capability and range increased once he could drive. Locally he relied on people he knew to tell him where planes had crashed. After discovering most of the crash sites in southern Rhode Island, he turned to areas surrounding military bases in

Massachusetts, New Hampshire, and Maine, which were unfamiliar territory. "In the town where the base is located, I checked the death records during World War II. The records don't report plane crashes. I looked for military officers who had died of 'multiple lacerations.'" He then checked a local newspaper on that date and very often found that a plane had crashed.

The combination of losing a job and the gas crunch of the early 1970s curtailed his expeditions to the north. Also around that time towns had begun to seal their death records.

After 1972 he took vacations to search for downed aircraft in Washington and Florida. In Florida, just south of Cape Canaveral, he and a local crash hunter conducted a search from the air in a T-6, a restored World War II plane, "a real treat." He was glad that such treats were infrequent, however, as he was prone to airsickness and hated to fly. "I've seen and studied too many crashes," he said.

At the time of his 1988 return to the swamp, Larry was working as a mechanical engineer designing printing presses. He referred to himself as an "aviation archaeologist." Several friends, though, nicknamed him "the aluminum undertaker."

In his backyard, a snow fence enclosed the fruits of his archaeological digs: forty thousand pounds of metal, glass, and rubber — bits and pieces of crashed airplanes. Most of the pieces were metal, much of it a dull silver color, exposed to the elements for 25 or more years. (There's a tendency to use *pieces* and *parts* interchangeably in describing what was back there. But parts can fit back together; crumpled, jagged, twisted, mangled pieces cannot.) Identifiable items included twisted 20-mm cannon, fuselage sections, wings, tail assemblies, propellers, landing gear, tires, canopies, and engines.

"There's a story behind every crash," Larry told a visitor, standing next to a pile of small metal pieces among the shrubs. Each pile represented (or totaled, equaled, or was all that was left of) a single plane. Generally, the smaller the pieces were, the more violent the crash. The pieces in this particular pile were small. "The engine from that plane is still buried eight feet in the ground."

Sometimes the best story lay not in the crash but in Larry's salvage efforts. In April 1944, two weeks after the two Hellcats collided over South Kingston, an F6F-3N night fighter crashed into the Pawcatuck River in Richmond. He began digging in the riverbank in 1964. Up to his waist in mud, he thought he felt the pilot's helmet with his foot. "I struggled to get it up," he said. "It was a giant snapping turtle."

The two types of planes usually flown in the area, the F6F-series Hellcat and SB2C-series Helldiver, accounted for the largest portion of total wreckage in the backyard. But there were fragments from many other types of aircraft.

"Let's see, er . . . what rubble have I picked up?" Larry thrived on the challenge of listing his inventory: SBD-4 Dauntless, P-47D Thunderbolt, AD-2/-3/-5 Skyraider (he was a stickler on getting the numbers correct), F4U-1-4 Corsair, TBM-3 Avenger, F3D-2 Skynight, S-2 Tracker, F-89 Scorpion, F-86 Saber jet, PT-23 Cornell trainer, A4D-2 Skyhawk, AF-2 Guardian, F8F-1 Bearcat. He claimed to know where all the pieces were located. "I have the type of mind that does two things very well: I know how things fit together, and I remember where things are."

He received calls regularly from people around the country who were restoring World War II aircraft, asking whether he had a particular part. (Aircraft restorers, with a lot of work, time, and skill, fashion parts out of pieces.) Larry usually knew right away whether he had it.

Larry's collection was an invaluable resource for World War II aircraft restorers. A North Dakota man restoring a World War II F4U-4 fighter visited him during the late 1980s. "His eyes lit up when he saw what I have. The parts he got from me saved him months of work."

Larry, too, benefitted from the wreckage. He devoted a decade and a half to restoring a Hellcat, subsequently put on display at the New England Air Museum at Bradley International Airport in Windsor Locks Connecticut. He possessed a wealth of information on many World War II aircraft, but he spoke of the Hellcat with special awe. "The Hellcat saved the Pacific. It had the highest kill ratio of any military aircraft, 18:1." He read books on the topic (the best new ones were coming from Japan), talked to ex-Hellcat pilots, and bought a videotape of the movie *Flying Leathernecks* from John Wayne. When Grumman, the company that manufactured the plane, would receive inquiries about the Hellcat, they would call Larry.

Of the 12,200 Hellcats that Grumman built from 1939 to 1946, only 20 existed by the late 1980s. Six were in flying condition, and the rest were in museums. Larry's Hellcat, which would never fly, was unique because it contained all original components — the only one in the world "historically accurate." Many of its parts came from 9B.

Larry located the wreckage of 9A in August 1963. Although it had crashed in the middle of the swamp, metal salvagers had been there first (in the late 1950s, Larry speculated) and had already removed the wings, fuselage, and tail section. The find still proved valuable, however, as he recovered assorted instrumentation from the cockpit.

Larry had expected to find 9B that same year. While there was no consensus on the plane's exact location or that it even existed, he concentrated his search to the east of 9A because of what several people had told him, including his grandmother, the only person he knew of who had actually witnessed the midair collision.

While Larry was a student at the University of Rhode Island in the late 1960s, he searched for 9B every winter vacation and on many winter weeekends. Searching in the summer was impossible — the swamp vegetation was too thick to walk or see through. But the more he searched, the more he doubted that 9B had crashed there.

Critical information came to him one Saturday in May 1969 while he was on an underwater dig in Worden's Pond, a large pond in South Kingston once used by the navy for dive-bombing practice. A Hellcat dive-bomber had crashed there in 1945. With his rowboat anchored in three feet of water, Larry had been walking in the muck, feeling for pieces. He filled the boat until it nearly sank.

That Saturday a man in his sixties paddled over to him in a canoe, and Larry told him what he was doing. "Have you heard about the Blue Star Boys?" the man asked. Larry hadn't. The Blue Star Boys had been a group of local teenagers during World War II who rode to crash sites on their bicycles, the man told him. He mentionerd a name — Bob Eaton.

Larry located Bob Eaton through his parents in Peacedale, Rhode Island. Living in Washington state, Bob was by then a retired air force mechanic who had served in Vietnam. His job had included investigating air crashes.

Eaton replied quickly to Larry's letter, recalling not only the two Hellcats that had collided over South Kingston but also the visit he and the other Blue Star Boys had made to the 9A crash site the next day. While trying to unbolt one of the machine guns, he had slipped and badly cut his forearm. But he also wrote that 9B was not worth seeing. Nothing was left. Larry wrote back saying he wanted to see for himself. Could he give him directions? Bob's next letter mentioned the two key landmarks: the end of the stone wall and a very tall white pine.

The bull briers were sharp. The goose-down parka that Larry's companion was wearing in the swamp looked as though it has been attacked by a cat. With less than half an hour of daylight left, Larry finally found his 19-year-old trail — an occasional branch sawed off at knee level. He had not wanted other hunters to discover 9B in those early years, yet he also was making many trips back and forth to the plane.

Thirty yards down the trail he stopped. He had found the tall white pine. It was dead, its upper third felled by the wind, but what remained of its thick, bleached-white trunk was taller than any nearby tree. Twenty years earlier, Larry recalled, the tree had been topped with an osprey nest. He looked round. Ten feet away was the other landmark, the stone wall. In the timelessness of the swamp, the old memories came back, hard and fresh.

"First I saw the tree, then I saw the end of the wall. I knew I was *very* close. But I still didn't see the plane. Right about here" — he kicked aside leaves — "I saw the first piece."

Larry kicked at a piece of rubber half buried in the leaves. At a quick glance it looked like a shredded automobile tire. "That's part of the fuel tank. They were made of rubber."

He walked around a few steps. "It still took me about an hour to find the plane. That's how well it was hidden. I walked this way." Bending low he entered a rhododendron grove and came to a crater about eight feet in diameter, no telling how deep, filled with water and covered by a skim of ice. Fragments of metal, tubing, and rubber lay around its sandy perimeter. Surrounded by tall rhododendrons, it was a cool, quiet, private room.

Squatting close to the ground Larry said in a soft voice, "The whole plane was right here. The tail was up in the air. Nobody had touched it. The engine is still down there."

The Blue Star Boys had, in fact, been here, Larry learned from Bob Eaton. It had taken them several months to find it, but the smell and sight had turned them away immediately. Larry did not care to talk about human remains in detail. "That's where I buried the pilot." He pointed to the spot. He and his hiking companion let it rest at that.

5

SCHEMERS

M. ROBERT BEASLEY

The Man Who Drove a Million People Crazy

FROM CANADA TO the Gulf of Mexico, from the Atlantic Ocean to the Mississippi River, a million people clothed in flowing white robes gathered on hilltops and in cemeteries. While flames from huge bonfires leaped high, they prayed, sang hymns, and prostrated themselves, jibbering, muttering, sobbing. At midnight all faces turned toward the sky, expecting to see it burst open and all true believers — living and dead — called into the paradise of heaven. The remaining world and sinners would then be destroyed by fire.

This was the hour of the Great Reckoning, October 22, 1844. The million fanatics, who had destroyed their homes, thrown their money and valuables into the streets, and now stood awaiting entrance into heaven, were Millerites. This group of feverishly religious people, who gave the world one of its largest and most grotesque displays of mass hysteria, was inspired by one man — a self-styled preacher named William Miller.

Born into a conservative Massachusetts family in 1782, Miller displayed an unusual interest in books and studies from an early age. Upon reaching manhood he turned atheist, calling all religious rites superstitions and humbug. He later joined the army and witnessed so much suffering and death in battle that he converted back to religion. He also suffered a leg injury. En route to a hospital he fell from the wagon, landing on his head. He was unconscious for several days but recovered physically, leaving the service in June 1815.

Believing in his religious conversion that the Lord was trying to convey a message to him, he devoted 14 years exclusively to biblical research, specifically seeking the secret of death and the hereafter. Using the periods referred to as 2,300 days, the "seven times" Gentile supremacy, and the 1,335 days in the Book of Daniel as prophetic periods, he concluded that Judgment Day would occur between March 21, 1843, and March 21, 1844.

In 1831 he received his first message "direct from God": "Go tell your findings to the world."

"I can't," he replied, "for I have no way of meeting people."

"That will be arranged," said the voice from heaven.

A half hour later a messenger arrived from Dresden, telling him that the local preacher had suddenly been stricken ill and requesting him to speak from the pulpit that morning. *This was it!* A way had been opened to deliver his message.

After informing the congregation that Judgment Day was approaching, he cautioned them that before his prophecy could be fulfilled, four definite signs must occur:

1. Wonders would be seen in the skies.

2. The earth would tremble in various places throughout the world.

3. There would be war among mankind.

4. Man would show marked intelligence in earthly progress.

As if by divine power, the signs began to appear:

1. On November 1, 1833, thousands of brilliant stars were seen falling from the skies and balls of fire blazed in the zenith for 50 minutes.

2. Earthquakes were reported in England, India, the West Indies, and various other countries.

3. Numerous revolutions began breaking out in Europe.

4. Mankind had displayed unprecedented intelligence during the previous few years, resulting in an unparalleled inventive and industrial expansion.

This resolved all doubts, and the Millerite cult expanded.

Miller personally delivered several thousand speeches throughout the East, while a thousand other preachers joined forces to spread the Word. Miller's dynamic speaking power was shown in Portland, Maine. After a lecture there in 1841, booksellers sold more Bibles in one month than they had during the previous 10 years!

As the critical period approached and the impending cataclysm seemed inevitable, people were again aroused to participate in feverish mass demonstrations when solar halos appeared over Danville, Kentucky, on January 4, 1843, followed shortly by another fiery display over New York City. Loved ones who died were not buried but were carried to camps so they might all ascend into heaven together. Betrothed girls refused to complete the marital agreement so they might enter heaven as virgins. Numerous cases were reported in which fanatical devotees killed their entire families and themselves, believing that the dead would be resurrected into heaven first. Individual suicides were a daily occurrence, and hospitals and mental institutions accepted capacity loads.

A woman in Windsor, Connecticut, believing she had been in direct communication with the Lord and had acquired supernatural powers, tried to walk across the river — and immediately drowned. Another enthusiast, saying he possessed celestial powers, drove his horse and buggy over a cliff only to learn that he didn't possess such powers — and was splattered all over the hillside.

Then came the final straw. The biggest ball of fire ever to approach the earth was seen when the Great Comet of 1843 appeared in the sky. Even confirmed atheists trembled at this blazing spectacle. This phenomenon more than doubled the believers flocking into Millerite camps.

The day after this fiery display, Miller published a statement in the *New York Herald* that the destruction of the world by fire would take place April 3, 1843. Ironically, Miller was stricken ill at a mass meeting on April Fool's Day 1843. Even while semiconscious he continued babbling, "I shall see Christ this year!"

On April 3 at Westford, Massachusetts, a zealous group of Millerites gathered at the famous Bancroft mansion prior to assembly on the hilltops for ascension. The mansion had been stripped bare of furniture to provide fuel for the bonfires, and thousands of believers were gathered inside fervently praying.

Typical of many small towns, Westford had a village idiot, Crazy Amos. Because of his obvious mental shortcomings, Amos was not a member of the Millerites, but he was not to be outdone. As the Bancroft mansion was filled to overflowing, he secured a large horn and let out several earsplitting blasts on the front lawn.

Thinking the horn was a summons by Gabriel, the worshippers

tumbled from doors and windows, shouting, "Hallelujah! Glory to God! The time has come!"

"You fools! Go dig your potatoes!" screamed Crazy Amos. "Angel Gabriel won't go a-diggin' 'em for you!"

April 3, 1843, passed uneventfully, and the earth, instead of being swept by fire, donned garments of spring and burst into leaf and song. The Millerites consoled themselves with the belief that the original prophecy had stated that Judgment Day would come sometime *between* March 1843 and March 1844. They turned to prayer, still convinced that the fiery end was near.

On March 21, 1844, the final date of the unexpected ending of the world, they again gathered, praying through the night and, expecting to be snatched momentarily into heaven. But again dawn broke as usual, and, unmindful of Miller's prophecy of coming destruction, the earth continued its normal course.

Slowly and silently the groups disbanded, their eyes filled with tears, their hearts heavy. Their white robes were soiled and torn; they were hungry and exhausted. But where could they go? They had no homes or worldly goods and were now faced with the urgency of finding food, clothing, and shelter, for the bitter winds of March did not share their fanatical faith.

Miller, who had remained at his Massachusetts home for the crucial hour of judgment, spent several days checking calculations, then announced that the error had been located. He had used the Gregorian calendar instead of the Jewish one, which put him seven months off in his figures. The Great Day was *certain* to take place on October 22!

Couriers were sent to his thousand ministers. "Our faith has been tested! By rechecking calculations, and through spiritual messages I have received, I humbly announce as a faithful disciple, that the Second Advent of Christ will occur October 22nd, 1844. Prepare yourself for this Great Day!" Incredible as it sounds, after two dates had proved failures, Millerites gathered back into the fold with renewed fervor, and thousands of new converts were added.

A woman in South Coventry, Connecticut, was said to have died following 10 years of illness. After doctors had pronounced her dead, she had returned to life. For the next 12 days she ate no food, only drinking two cups of weak tea daily, and spent all her time loudly singing hymns. At all meetings this woman was held before them as an example of miracles being performed on earth, since she was reported to have said she was returned from the dead to await Judgment Day.

At one such meeting in Philadelphia, a group of young men, not under the influence of fanatical fever, surrounded the meeting hall. At a given signal, every window in the building was broken simultaneously and firecrackers were tossed into the room. The wind whistled through the smashed windows, extinguishing the candles and lamps, and the firecrackers began exploding in the dark, Millerite-packed room. Several of them were trampled to death, and many others were seriously injured in making a mass exodus from what appeared to have been the wrong direction in their ascension.

On October 22 the now familiar pattern was repeated. Every hilltop and cemetery was jammed with white-robed figures huddled around huge bonfires, praying and chanting hymns. A perverse group had even gathered where a mass execution of "witches" had previously been conducted.

One farmer in New Haven, Connecticut, gathered his family in the living room on that fateful night. Looking out his window, he saw the night sky ablaze. Believing the time had finally arrived, he killed his family of five and then himself, with only the servant girl escaping. He never realized that what caused the sky to be illuminated was not the coming of Judgment Day but his neighbor's house and barn burning to the ground.

The night of October 22 passed without the prophesied destruction. Dawn found pathetic, disillusioned groups, wet from rains of the night, cold from October winds, and broken in mind, body, and spirit. Not only were they still earthly mortals, but since they had destroyed their worldly possessions, they were poverty-stricken mortals.

The task of beginning life over was too much for many to face. Thousands of suicides and family slaughters occurred. Hospitals and asylums were unable to accommodate the unprecedented number of mental cases.

Through all the agony, poverty, insanity, and suicides, Miller reposed comfortably and securely at his luxurious farm. What the fanatical Millerites overlooked was that in April 1843, when Miller had first predicted the ending of the world, he had just installed 40 rods of new stone fence on his property. On the October date, when he positively confirmed the destruction of all things worldly, he had a full woodshed and pantry, while his fields and livestock were well tended. Such preparations for the future certainly cast suspicion on the sincerity of a man who prophesied complete oblivion for mankind. They also overlooked the fact that at each of the meetings enormous collections, many times consisting of diamonds, gold, and entire life savings in cash, which he said would be of no value, were taken up.

During the next five years Miller lived as a recluse, gradually going blind. Possibly the head injury in 1818 had finally caught up with him, for his years of marked mental deterioration developed into complete insanity before his death in 1849 at Low Hampton, New York. With his dying breath he still tried to incite others with his delusions, crying out, "Victory! At last I see Him!"

Perhaps his million followers could have been spared their poverty, hardship, insanity, and untimely deaths had they studied the same Bible a little further and read the recorded words of St. Matthew in speaking of Judgment Day: "But of that day and hour knoweth no man, no, not even the Angels in Heaven."

The Witch
of Wall Street

HETTY GREEN DIDN'T HAVE much use for money, though she was one of the richest women in the world. For Hetty money was something to get and to have but not to spend. Born in 1835 to a wealthy New Bedford, Massachusetts, family, she inherited five million or so and managed to make it grow by being the most perfect of misers, the Scrooge of Scrooges.

The future "Witch of Wall Street" made her first killing in the booming bonds of the post–Civil War years. At that time she also acquired a millionaire husband, Edward Green, whom she sent packing in 1885 for his spendthrift ways. He died in 1902 with seven dollars and a gold watch to his name.

Hetty kept their two children on short rations and in second-hand clothes. As a result, her son Edward lost a leg to gangrene when Hetty balked at paying a doctor; her daughter Sylvia was made a nun because convents didn't charge room and board.

Hetty Green's financial dealings were instinctive, brilliant, and preternaturally profitable. She became a familiar figure on Wall Street, striding up and down in a rotting black dress and rubber boots stuffed with millions in cash and securities. She lived in hovels and dined in dives. No economy was too small for Hetty. She bought newspapers for two cents and resold them for one; she hunted all over town for a misplaced stamp; she once spent hours searching a street for a coin her son had lost.

Her last years were increasingly haunted by fears that somebody would get her money at last. Her banker was trying to poison her, she said. The tax collectors were after her, or the lawyers or doctors. She outwitted them all. Hetty died in 1916 a hundred million in the black. The queen of skinflints made her most expensive journey posthumously when her body was shipped back to Bellows Falls, Vermont, to be buried in the family plot.

HERBERT ADAMS

The Saga of Nature Man

THE NAKED MAN stood in the midst of the Maine wilderness, ringed with reporters. Scornfully he flung aside a final cigarette; staunchly he faced the dark woods. "See you later, boys!" he boomed and manfully marched forth into the forest primeval.

"AND NAKED HE PLUNGES INTO THE WOODS," headlined the breathless *Boston Post*, "TO LIVE ALONE TWO MONTHS!"

Thus began the saga of Joe Knowles, the "Nature Man." On August 4, 1913, the 43-year-old Maine native shucked both shirt and civilization and took to the woods, he proclaimed, to seek the title of our modern world's first "Primitive Man" and to prove our pampered race was still master of its fate. For two months

Knowles — bold as Daniel Boone, clever as Robinson Crusoe — thrilled *Boston Post* readers with tales of his two-fisted fights with bears, bull moose, and evil elements.

Two months later, On October 4, Knowles burst out of the Canadian forest — bronzed, bearded, clad in bearskin, backpacking a fire-making machine — into the glare of Lindbergh-like adulation from coast to coast. Ahead lay fame, fortune, pretty girls, a vaudeville tour, a bestselling book, and squads of skeptics who screamed the whole thing was a spectacular hoax.

Did Joe Knowles, in fact, fool Dame Fortune but not Mother Nature? Even today, the Nature Man, though grown somewhat shaggy, remains a mystery.

But for millions of readers in 1913, that last giddy summer before the Great World War, Joe was a spiritual symbol of the age, a parable in bearskin. For millions more he was a faker of Falstaffian proportions, a Barnum of the backwoods. Either way, for the *Boston Post* Joe was a colossal success, because the great debate hurt newspaper sales — soon soaring higher than sea gulls above Beacon Hill — not one whit.

Yes, the whole episode had its "unusual and mysterious side," Joe would say with a smile much later, when sporting cigars and three-piece suits. "Probably all of us have wild dreams now and then. I am beginning to think wild dreams are wonderful things to have."

As a boy Joe Knowles ran away from home and, in a sense, kept going all his life. Born in Wilton, Maine, in 1869, the son of a Civil War soldier, Joe quarreled with his invalid father but idolized his half-Indian mother. The sole support of her family, the resourceful woman wove baskets, chopped wood, and once fed her snowbound brood of six for three days on a single turkey egg. "She was the most courageous person I ever met," Joe said.

At 13 Joe ran away to sea, served a hitch in the navy, and sailed the Great Lakes, where, he later claimed, Sioux and Chippewa warriors taught him woodcraft. A talented but untrained artist, Joe returned to Maine and made a living of sorts painting and guiding around the town of Eustis. Joe never exactly burned with ambition, recalled Helon Taylor, then a boy in Eustis and later superintendent of Maine's Baxter State Park. "Awfully lazy," said Taylor, "but couldn't he draw!"

In 1912 the "wild idea" struck Joe while he was painting the portrait of a Vermont moose. "It hit me hard," said Joe. Not hard enough for William Randolph Hearst's *Boston American,* home of many a well-financed publicity stunt, which turned Joe down cold. So he went to the moribund *Boston Post,* his part-time artistic employer, which embraced what bloomed — to the amazement of all — into one of the oddest episodes in American journalism.

The plan: Joe would march into the Maine woods, with nary a match nor a stitch, and live alone on wits and woodcraft for 60 days. He would seek no help and see no one, and no one would see him. The place: north of Flagstaff Lake, in the forbidding Dead River region of northwest Maine, near the ragged border with Canada. Joe's daily diary, scrawled in charcoal on birch bark, would be dropped at a secret spot to edify the outside world. "I wanted to get away from the sham of modern life," said Joe. "Time and again I said to myself, 'Here is a chance to show you are a man.'"

Alas, what a man. Pale and pudgy, a chain-smoker, Joe was nobody's idea of Adonis. Dr. Dudley Sargent of Harvard examined the 5-foot 9-inch, 200-pound Knowles and tactfully suggested that "his considerable fat . . . should aid him in resisting the cold."

Undaunted, Joe and two dozen newsmen and well-wishers gathered in the August drizzle below Bear Mountain, by King and Bartlett Lake, north of Eustis. At 10 A.M., tastefully attired in an athletic supporter (dropped out of camera range), Joe shared harrdshakes and a final smoke, bid adieu to civilization, and struck out eastward through the wilds toward lonely Spencer Lake. The drizzle turned into a downpour, and as Knowles trudged off down the trail, says one account, "the mosquitoes must have buzzed with glee."

Days of dismal rain later, Joe awoke one morning hungry, homesick, and still naked as a newborn, with a vision of his mother before him. It was his 44th birthday, and only the memory of his mother — that wizard with turkey eggs — drove him on. Wrote Joe, "My mother had no use for a quitter."

Nor, presumably, did the *Boston Post.* Thus inspired, Joe was soon weaving grass leggings and cedar-bark moccasins and dining on berries by a cozy campfire, started Boy Scout fashion with a friction firebox. Daily he sallied forth to catch trout barehanded ("The simplest thing in the world"); nightly he sketched forest scenes on fungus and scribbled his adventures on birch bark. Twice a week Joe tucked his birch-bark dispatches into the roots of an overturned spruce near Spencer Lake and merrily marched back to his bare-knuckled battle with the wilderness.

Rain or shine, stoic Joe strode naked between sturdy lean-tos near Horseshoe Bog and Lost Pond because "fresh air makes rich red blood, and rich red blood makes a healthy brain" — and besides, cedar-bark skirts "when wet, tear easily." It was honor above all for Joe, who shared his warm bed with a black snake and saved a weak fawn from a beastly bruin. Joe kept partridges as pets (after cooking their cousins) who "playfully pecked at my hand and danced coyly along, exactly as a woman who says no when she means yes."

At the end of the first week Joe felt like the Caveman Compleat. "I wonder if my mother could have recognized me," he gloried, gazing happily at his grizzled reflection in a pool. "I felt strong enough to pull up a tree by the roots. I was, in truth, a Primitive Man."

Delighted, the bonanza-minded *Boston Post* moved Joe to page one and dubbed him "The American Adam . . . the Rip Van Winkle of the Wilderness." Across the craze-happy country Joe moved to center stage. Bookmakers beamed; whole families argued. And upon the *Post* their letters fell like autumn leaves, full of advice, prayers, and proposals of marriage.

Meanwhile, as fall came, Joe worked his way up the food chain, knocking off partridges with his homemade bow of hornbeam and reluctantly wrestling a deer to its doom by pouncing upon it and wringing its neck. "I want to apologize for killing the deer in that manner," Joe confessed, comfy in his new buckskin chaps, "but under the circumstances, it was the only way I had."

Readers next gasped at Joe's crowning glory: enticing a bear into a clever pitfall. Joe conked it on the nose with his hornbeam club and with boiled bark tanned himself a handsome new shawl. "Why, there isn't an animal in the forest that doesn't want to make friends with man!" wrote Joe, munching on bear meat. The master predator then relaxed by rolling whitewood-leaf cigarettes. "Not because I wanted to smoke particularly," he piously noted, "but out of mere curiosity, as I had a few idle moments to spare." He missed salt, Joe admitted, but mostly he was lonely.

All this and much more bedazzled readers of the *Boston Post*, which doubled its circulation to 200,000 in two months. Across the nation syndication services snapped Joe up. Suddenly Woodrow

Wilson went unnoticed, the Panama Canal made dull plodding, drought-stricken North Anson, Maine, burned down—all humdrum fare. From barrooms to brokerage houses the nation's eager eyes turned to lonely Joe Knowles, the "Naked Thoreau."

As did the cold eyes of the Maine Fish and Game Commissioners, who had refused Joe permission to kill game out of season, much less in print. Late in September Joe was seized by an obsessive fear that wardens would haul him from the forest, stripped of skins before his time was up. "I grew revengeful at this thought. The idea that I was hunted brought out the animal in me," warned Joe. "My mind was filled with wardens." In a final note Joe announced that he would emerge from the woods at Lake Megantic, Quebec, far from the long arm of the U.S. law.

A 4 P.M. on October 4, 1913—guided north, he noted, by moss on the trees—Joe stepped onto the tracks of the Canadian Pacific Railroad and flagged down a freight train. "Not knowing who I might meet," Joe had modestly donned his bristling bearskin, and children screamed and fled at the sight. But at Megantic a booming international welcome awaited the Primitive Man, replete with brass bands, bunting, bevies of British and American officials, and four genial Maine game wardens, come to escort Joe home. "Never felt finer in my life," Joe smiled to surging reporters. "Say, is there a cigarette around here?"

Thanks to the *Post's* public relations wizard, Paul V. Waitt, Joe's return to Boston was worthy of a Roman general. Resplendent in his bearskin, riding a private railroad coach, Joe greeted roaring crowds at every tank town and city en route from Quebec to Beantown. At Wilton a cornet band and parade of six hundred marched Joe to a tearful reunion with his mother. At Lewiston thousands launched "Three cheers for Joe Knowles, who fought and won!" At Portland ten thousand turned out, and Mayor Curtis annointed Joe with the dubious honor of "demonstrating that modern man is the equal of man of the Stone Age."

At Augusta hundreds jammed the statehouse, where a closed-door meeting of the Fish and Game Commissioners slapped Joe with a $205 fine for such sundry offenses as "illegal cooking fires." To the end of his life Joe resented it. "Such is the condition of the state of Maine today!" growled the Naked Thoreau.

Near the end, Waitt remembered, the famous bearskin grew so ripe that Joe donned it "with great resignation" and wearily went forth to greet his public while holding his nose.

On October 9, some 150,000 (by official estimates) turned out for Joe's triumphant return to the *Boston Post* (which counted the crowd at 400,000) and a roaring noon reception on Boston Common. At Harvard Dr. Sargent reexamined Joe, declaring he had lost 11 pounds, expanded his lung capacity, and developed "the Perfect Skin . . . as a result of wind, weather, and sunlight." At Cambridge, four hundred college girls serenaded Joe and filed blushingly by to touch the "Perfect Skin."

On and on, like Indian summer, the warm adulation glowed. "Old Fogeyism will not do in the woods or in the church! boomed the pastor of Boston's Warren Avenue Church. "Behold Joe Knowles, a sermon two months long for the people of the United States!"

Behold indeed, Filene's proclaimed, inviting the public to witness its downtown department store go Darwin one better, putting Joe "through the process of Evolution from Primitive to Modern Man . . . including manicure and fashionable clothes from our Fine Men's Shops."

Joe signed for a multiweek vaudeville tour, variously reported at $400 to $1,200 a week, and even found time to marry Miss Marion Humphrey of Dedham, onstage, one memorable night. In jig time, with Waitt's help, Joe turned out an epic autobiography, *Alone In the Wilderness: by Joseph Knowles*. In the bookstores by December, dedicated (of course) "To My Mother," it sold 300,000 copies. Lean on woodcraft but long on philosophy, in between battles with bull moose, Joe opined on kids ("So long as they keep screaming, they are all right"), wives ("I'd make her come up to my ideal"), and red-blooded American boyhood. "Boys," wrote Joe, fresh in Filene's finest, "you should always ask yourself: Am I making the most of what I have?"

But thunder was brewing in the corporate wilds. It was not nice to fool Mother Nature, but it was worse to cross William Randolph Hearst, whose *Boston American* now broadsided the Nature Man with embarrassing exposés. Furious at losing the stunt of the century, Hearst minions fanned into the forest, turning up fishy facts and odd characters galore, like Dead River denizen "Tripe" Demming, who claimed an Indian pal had shot Joe's famous bear. Worse yet, he winked, a girl had warmed Joe's lean-to weekly, and in a guarded cabin at Spencer Lake Joe hid below the floorboards when not playing cards with his cronies.

In vain the *Post* fired back. "I feel pity, not anger, toward critics who do not believe, simply because they do not know," said Joe loftily, slapping a $50,000 lawsuit on Hearst. Still, Joe's stock dropped dramatically (though Demming recanted when Hearst reneged on a hushed-up $1,000 payoff), and from the stage of Boston's Tremont Temple Joe declared that he would return to the wilds to prove he wore his laurels legitimately.

In midwinter Joe trudged back out of Eustis before the strangest safari in Maine history. All sensible Maine bears were asleep, so a 250-pound bruin was captured in Canada, shipped to Portland, and hauled overland by Joe, puffing reporters, and a notary public, back to the bear pit at Lost Pond. "It was the middle of December with 12 inches of snow on the ground," recalled 15-year-old Helon Taylor, who tagged along. "The bear wasn't doing very well. He'd had a long trip and wanted to hibernate."

After dumping the bedraggled bruin in the pit, Joe dispatched him with one blow and set to work with a sharp rock. "In less than 10 minutes he had the hide off one leg," said Taylor. "We were all impressed."

So far so good, but marching home by Joe's haunts at Lost Pond, the startled witnesses spied a nice new log cabin "with a pile of beer bottles and tin cans about four feet high out behind it." Joe hotly denied he'd ever seen it. "But Lost Pond is small and round, and· I don't think there was one spot on shore from which you couldn't see that camp," said the crestfallen Taylor. "Joe was lying to us. I lost all faith in him right there."

There was more suspicious evidence, like bullet holes in Joe's cedar-bark packbasket, said Taylor. "That bothered me before, but the Lost Pond camp clinched it. He was a fake."

For the Nature Man it was all downhill from there. In 1914, this time at the behest of Hearst's *San Francisco Examiner*, Joe marched nude into Oregon's wild Siskiyou Mountains. Eight days later World War I broke out, and the kaiser kicked Joe Knowles back into the comic pages.

In 1916 Joe tried again in upper New York, training a "Dawn Woman" in "Dawn Man" woodcraft. Amid much ballyhoo the "Dawn Duo" set out into the forest — separately, of course. After a week of rain, Dawn Woman went home, taking most of the publicity with her. Disgusted, Joe pulled on his pants for good and trudged off into the thickets of anonymity.

Decades later the memory of this fallen hero still hurt Helon Taylor. "Joe was a great woodsman and could have done everything he said he did. My big regret is that he didn't, " sighed Taylor in 1973. "And I don't know why. Too lazy, I guess. Too bad."

Joe died in 1942, still a dreamer, in a driftwood shack he built on the shores of Washington state — appropriately, near Cape Disappointment. "It would have been a knockout — parading out of that timber a-leading a bear cub like a Scottie," he once sighed, a showman to the end. "It's about the only regret I have," he said, "that and the goddamn war breaking out when it did!"

6

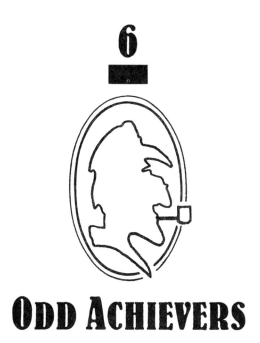

ODD ACHIEVERS

Hardworking Hands

In New York City one day in the mid-1980s Laurence White saw his hands caressing a woman's feet and holding a glass of Cutty Sark whiskey in the subway, pouring a glass of Labatt's beer at a bus stop, holding a bottle of Miller beer on the bus, and turning on a Sony television set in Times Square. Laurence earned a living by modeling his hands. They appeared in magazines, on billboards, and on television. His hands were in advertisements for Ivory soap, Nivea cream, IBM computers, Post Raisin Bran cereal, Liquid Tide, MasterCard, van Cleef diamonds, Polaroid cameras, Schrade hunting knives, Citizen watches, and many other well-known products.

"Sometimes," said Laurence, "I point to a billboard and say to a friend, 'You see those hands?' and my friend say, 'Yeah, are they yours?" I say, 'Nope, just seeing if you're awake.'"

Laurence worked mostly in New York, but he grew up in Hull, Massachusetts. He believed it was his destiny to become a hand model. The person with scarred hands, a slightly crooked finger, or an enlarged knuckle should not plan on hand modeling as a career. The hands of a hand model must appear as if they have grown-up in a pair of gloves. Before Laurence had ever considered that someone might want to take pictures of his hands, he had broken each finger at least once playing basketball. And in his early twenties, while attempting to establish a career as a fashion model in Boston, he had worked nights as a bartender, cutting and scraping his hands many times on the job. But his broken fingers had healed without a flaw and the cuts without a trace.

Pointing out that he had great-looking hands, Clint Clemens, a photographer in Boston, used Laurence's hands for the cover of the Spalding annual report in 1976. By then Laurence realized that his opportunities as a fashion model were limited. Those models in the highest demand had a midwestern look with fair skin and blue eyes, while he looked European with dark hair, dark eyes, and slightly olive skin. His hands, on the other hand, could take him to the top.

In 1978, then 24 years old, he moved to Munich, Germany, to launch his career as a hand model. As Paris is known for fashion photography, Munich is the European center for product photography. Two years later, having worked for a well-known European modeling agency and amassed an impressive portfolio, he moved to New York City, the world center for product photography. His first several years there were filled with frustration, as he had few jobs and little money.

Persistence paid off. After 16 rejections he was finally accepted by the exclusive Ford modeling agency. By the mid-1980s, said Laurence, the world's top three male hand models were working for the Ford agency: Greg Fortune, who specialized in television commercials; John Carthay, the top print-media hand model; and himself, also a print-media specialist. The three of them, Laurence recalled, were "the workhorses of the business. . . . consistently used for the major advertising campaigns."

What made John Carthay number one and Laurence White, as he liked to call himself, "the Avis of hand models," number two? Or for that matter, what was so special about Laurence White's hands to begin with?

Nice moons. Laurence's moons looked like perfect arches drawn by an architect. Furthermore, his hands had good symmetry and were a good size and shape: not too big, not too small. He wore size 10 gloves. His thumb and forefinger especially were well formed. "The thumb and forefinger are where it's at in product photography," he said, noting that they generally hold the product. Laurence's hands did not have much hair (the rest of his body is quite hairy), and his skin was smooth. He considered himself lucky. "I got my mother's hands."

However, hand modeling requires more than having physically attractive hands. It demands strength, flexibility, and a tolerance for pain. Laurence could hold a product in a position without moving for up to 30 minutes while the photographer snapped hundreds of photos, varying camera angles and lighting. "Under enormous strain, your hands must look comfortable and relaxed.

A pencil can bring you to your knees if you have to hold it a certain way." He was nicknamed "the human Gumby" for the contorted positions he could assume and hold. He spoke of different stages of discomfort he would feel in his hands and arms: "First they cramp, then they tingle, then they burn, then they go numb. After that, it's called Zen. You see God. I've screamed before, I've cursed, I've sweated, and I've shook, but my hands never moved."

The hand model also must know how to hold a product. That sounds simple, but Laurence would say it's not. "It's knowing how the product looks best. Your hand is secondary. After years and years of experience, you are able to *be* the product."

What, then, separated the two professionals, John Carthay and Laurence? John's thumbnail was square and Laurence's was round, for one thing.

"Squareness," said Laurence, speaking of how the advertising world views it, "connotes luxury and power. Roundness connotes athletics. Each of us gets certain types of jobs consistently. He does Piaget watches; I do Citizen. He does American Express; I do MasterCard."

Suffice it to say that both received handsome wages for their services. Hand modeling made Laurence a rich man — rich in the sense that he had free time. "To have time to read or to be able to sit in the park and listen to birds — that, to me, is being rich."

Laurence cared for his hands as though they were prize poodles. He had them professionally manicured weekly. Every morning, after showering, he washed his hands with Ivory soap, trimmed away loose cuticle with scissors, and then used a bleach stick under the nails to make them "look crisp, clean, and concise." After buffing the nails, he would put cream on his hands and wear gloves until it soaked in. In winter, when the air is very dry, he would often coat his hands with vitamin E oil and Vaseline at bedtime and then sleep with plastic bags on them.

He wore gloves outdoors year-round. Gloves protected his hands from scrapes, bruises, and sunlight. With olive skin, he could not afford the slightest tan on his hands. The advertising world, he said, "wants you to look like a business executive from Stamford, Connecticut. The whiter your hands, the better."

Because water can make the fingertips white and puffy, Laurence avoided swimming and bathtub immersions. Due to the high risk of hand injury, he gave up playing contact sports. Laurence missed playing basketball the most, but it was a sacrifice, one of many, he made to remain a top hand model. "I'm not a flash in the pan. This is a career. I'm willing to make concessions."

His whole lifestyle was a concession of sorts. "Being a hand model is like having a second conscience. You have to think before you do something as simple as open a door. Before opening a door, I wait several seconds to see whether somebody's going to open it from the other side."

His women friends adhered to certain ground rules. "She has to know what I do for a living, and that has a lot to do with what she can do. I remind her not to squeeze my hand. And there's never any scratching, even when she's playing." Laurence avoided other potential scratchers and biters: dogs, cats, and children.

He loved dancing but did none, fearing that his career could be ended on a dance floor where "people wear all sorts of jewelry and fling their arms around." Even a friendly handshake could be catastrophic. Laurence would first look at the hands. "You can tell a lot about a person by their hands. If someone is wearing jewelry or a particular type of watch, or the hands are dirty or have a cut or blister, or if a guy looks like 'Harry Bone Cruncher,' I won't shake hands with him."

Although he insured his hands against accidental injury with Lloyd's of London, there was one concession that he wouldn't make. He lifted weights six days a week, wearing five pairs of gloves to prevent calluses. As a result, he had muscular hands, and that excluded him from certain prestigious assignments. An advertisement for an ultra-expensive watch, for instance, would not have rugged-looking hands. But that was all right with Laurence. "Lifting weights puts my mind at peace, and when my mind is at peace, my hands are a peace."

Unlike models whose continued success depends on the shape of their bodies and faces, Laurence had a long career ahead of him. "A man's hand improves with age; it gets a worn, white Anglo-Saxon look," he observed. "If I take care of myself and my hands, I'll be in the business for 25 more years. . . . I love what I do and want to work for a living. I consider myself truly blessed in that sense."

His retirement fantasy, born from the incessant need to shelter and tend his hands, was to play basketball again, work with his hands again — and, the ultimate: "I'm going to shove my hands in a great bucket of slop and mush it around."

JAMES DODSON

The Killer Retired

ONE SUMMER MORNING during the mid-1980s at a rooftop restaurant overlooking Boston's Faneuil Hall marketplace, two men sat at a table talking. There were cut flowers on the white linen tablecloth, and brilliant sunlight streamed into the room.

"Let me get you to do something," said one of the men. His name was Walter, and he dwarfed everyone else in the restaurant. His hands were massive. His shoulders were possibly a yard wide, and his posture was slightly bowed. But his voice, which was deeply resonant, like a man speaking from a well, carried through the room.

"I want you," he said calmly, "to envision a great tree. Picture that tree spanning the continent, the ocean, the world. The entire world. Think about that tree a moment." He paused and sipped his grapefruit juice. "Now, let me ask you, if you desperately wanted to chop that tree down, how would you do it? You'd take up your little ax and start cutting away at it, right? But chances are you wouldn't make much progress. The work would overwhelm you."

At other tables, breakfast conversations stopped, and a few heads discreetly turned to regard this man. "Life is like that," Walter went ahead. "Say the tree is evil — it is everywhere, its roots extend to all places, it blots out the light around us. Light is power and energy. One man cannot remove this tree and let the light in." His voice intensified. "But think what would happen to that tree if, say, ten million little axes began to whittle away at it. That tree would know its days were numbered."

Walter smiled and sipped his juice again. People at the other tables looked blankly at one another. "Love is that kind of force," Walter continued, a little louder. He lightly pounded his fist on the

133

table, rattling the silverware. "It can bring down governments and rulers. Instead of criticizing our national leaders, if millions of Americans envisioned them surrounded by a pure postive light — the kind of love Christ taught, the kind Buddha taught — you would have a changed world. We are talking about" — he paused, inhaled, and exhaled — "*power*. Every human being has it within him. He just doesn't know how to unlock the door. He's never searched for the way. But I know. I've searched."

A businessman at a nearby table leaned over and shot him a nervous grin. Walter did not see him.

"The *power*," Walter said seriously, "is *love*. Pure love."

"Excuse me," the man said. His voice wobbled.

Walter turned. He frowned. "Yes?"

"Aren't you the Killer? Aren't you Killer Kowalski?"

Walter pursed his lips; his large head nodded modestly.

The man smiled, relieved. "I knew it was you. How you been, Killer? Whaddya doing these days? You still wrestling?"

"No. I retired."

"That's too bad. But you look great. I mean, I heard you talking and it threw me, but I knew it was the *Killer*." He said the name as if the words possessed a delicious illicit power. "I had to say something, because everybody knows the Killer."

Kowalski gave a small, tense smile. He seemed momentarily vexed by the interruption. He put on his spectacles and looked back at his companion. "Where were we?" he asked.

"Life. The power of love. Your search for peace."

Walter nodded. "Oh yes," he said, sighing. "The search. I've been searching my whole life. That's what life is, a journey, a search. You have to make it alone. You have to fix a picture of your own life in your head. There are three important keys: thought, feeling, and the spoken word. They're your God-given tools, but you have to find your way to peace."

There was a time not so long ago in an America starved for greater-than-life heroes when he was as close as you could get to the ultimate public villain. For almost 30 years Walter "Killer" Kowalski stalked professional wrestling rings all across America and around the world, twisting and bludgeoning his opponents in a brutal mayhem of flesh that made him one of the most loathed and feared men alive. When he entered sports arenas, women and children screamed their darkest thoughts at him; spectators hurled cabbages and rotten fruit and attacked him with chairs when he departed the ring. At the height of his career, the late 1950s and early 1960s, he received a thousand letters a week filled with the most venomous suggestions. There were death threats, lawsuits. he was shot at. Punks came at him with pocketknives. Small riots sometimes accompanied his appearances. On several occasions armed cops formed human walls to protect him. For a strange, turbulent golden time — almost a quarter of a century — Killer Kowalski dominated professional wrestling. He was the man America loved to hate most. He was America's premier antihero.

For a man who had his elbows and knees dislocated on several occasions, who had fingers wrenched from their sockets, ribs fractured, and his neck twisted to the point where his vertebrae nearly fused with his spine, he remained remarkably fit after his retirement from the ring. Walter Kowalski moved through the 1980s with a careful, patient grace. He was healed. Gone were the noisy arenas and death threats and top-drawer paychecks that made him, in an age before petulant six-figure superstars, one of the highest paid athletes in the world. After his last match in March 1977, Kowalski made a quiet living teaching wrestling to aspiring professionals — first at a school he started under his name at the Salem, Massachusetts, YMCA and later at the sooty YMC-Union on Boylston Street in Boston — and promoting wrestling shows on a small-time basis all around New England to benefit organizations such as police and firefighters' pension plans.

The Killer became just a memory, part of American myth. But the alter ego was a teacher who was very much alive. He wore eyeglasses and dressed conservatively. He drove a suburban station wagon with its radio tuned to classical music stations. By mixing religious philosophy with leg drops, he taught his wrestling students how to prevail in the ring and prosper in life. Most professional athletes, he contended, are like sheep when it comes to conducting their own lives. "They never think about who they are or what they are here for. They're willing to be led so easily. I try to tell them what to look out for. I know," he said, "because I've had those seductions. I've made the mistakes."

One afternoon in early July 1984 he had assembled four of his students on a dim, grimy stage on the third floor of the YMC-Union building. Buttery sunlight filtered through transom windows, and the sound of the street floated into the airy room. Walter

Kowalski was instructing his students on ring ethics. One of his students, a burly, bearded man named Richard, had come here from Providence. The afternoon before, Richard, a part-time employee of a light industrial service, had wrestled with a partner in a tag-team match promoted by Kowalski in Waltham. The partner, who was several years older and more established, had given Richard unsolicited advice throughout the match, and Richard had felt cheated of ring time, so he complained strenuously to his partner and to Walter Kowalski.

"Let me tell you something," Walter began quietly, holding a steady finger to his student's face. "You should listen to what everyone has to say to you. Maybe their advice isn't good, but maybe it's not that bad, either. You learn by listening and looking and keeping your mouth shut, *capiche?* You may hate the guy's guts, but what good is it going to do to tell him or to complain to somebody else about it? I tell you this: the guy who keeps his mouth shut and listens learns the most. He's the guy who goes furthest in life."

The other students — a young black man named Burt, a beefy red-haired teenager from Braintree named Chris, and a midget from Holbrook named Dana — formed a small, loose ring around their teacher, listening. Each student had worked out his own private financial terms with Kowalski. The process was remarkably democratic: some students paid a flat rate of about $1,000 for the benefit of instruction that could go on as long as a year before they would be ready for the ring; others, who couldn't afford the rate, paid less. A few paid nothing at all. "It all depends on the situation and the student," said Kowalski, who teaches about 20 students at any given time. "If some kid has the enthusiasm and the heart, as well as the raw talent, I can't refuse to teach him just because he can't come up with the cash right away. He may go on to be a great star."

"Ok," Kowalski said, "let's get going."

The wrestlers paired off and went through several standard maneuvers — scissors kicks, head holds, leg drops. The whole time Walter moved counterclockwise around the action, mumbling encouragement or barking, "No, no, nooooo." Once he stopped the proceedings between Chris and Burt. Chris was trying to learn a maneuver that required him to duck under his opponent's advancing arm, reverse his direction with a balletic spin, and take his opponent's legs out from under him. Kowalski walked through the move three times in a row, pausing with each strategic grip. "You *see*? This, *see*? He repeated "Not *there*. Not down there. That's *sloppy*." Each time Chris tried, he got it wrong. So Walter had Richard perform the move on him. The result: the Killer went slamming to the mat, sending powerful reverberations through the entire stage floor. For several seconds the Killer lay prone, motionless. Then he lifted his head, scowling in pain.

"I think you pinched a nerve," he growled. The students exchanged anxious glances. Richard offered the teacher a helping hand. The Killer seized the hand and flipped Richard over violently onto his back. Kowalski popped to his feet and grinned. The students looked stunned.

"Always expect the unexpected in life," Walter shouted. Then he relented, smiling again. "That's the message."

It is a variation of this same kind of violent tutelage that made Walter Kowalski a teacher in demand out of the ring also. He was frequently invited to speak to high school groups, civic organizations, and religious gatherings. In each instance his message was essentially the same: life is difficult but blessed; each person is his or her own divinity; you're bound to get tossed around on the wrestling mat of life, but that doesn't mean you'll lose the match. The power is entirely in your hands. You must learn how to locate it, focus it, and use it. The power is simple. The power is love. You have to picture it.

It was a tribute to something — Walter Kowalski's charisma or Killer Kowalski's enduring fame — that what he had to say, an obvious contradiction of the violent career behind him and the scripturally tender message he now preached, made such an impact on is audiences. They listened, even if they didn't hear. They would still ask him about the claw hold or the time he hurled Bruno Sammartino onto his head in a brutal match in Montreal. But there was an odd reverence visible in their faces. He was still larger than life to them.

Sometimes, life is a trick of optics. We somehow wind up appearing the opposite of what we are. At the beginning of his wrestling career, and certainly before, Walter Kowalski was one of the good guys. The youngest son of Polish immigrants, Walter grew up across the river from Detroit in Windsor, Canada. He was not born to become the world-famous Killer. He was born to become a student. At 12, scrawny — "like one of those punks advertised in the Charles Atlas ads" — and wanting to try out for the school swim team. He was devastated when a physician examined him and told his parents he had a heart murmur.

Walter went to the public library and checked out science books. In one book he read that proper nutrition could control the vagaries of health. He also read that the human heart was muscle, and he got to thinking about that, picturing it. At school a friend showed him a weight-lifting magazine. Walter put two and two together and came up with a strong heart. He *pictured* it in his head. He also read that eating animal flesh was a bad thing for spiritual as well as physical growth, so he devised a vegetarian menu and pasted it to his mother's refrigerator. "She thought I was crazy; the doctor thought I was crazy. They all did." He went down to the YMCA, joined up, and started lifting weights. Slowly he began to feel better.

A devout Catholic, he began to pray that he would soon get stronger. "Whenever I wanted something, I prayed for it. I visualized a blue sun above me — blue for wisdom — and lightning coming from it. A spiritual law holds that if you ask for understanding, it will not be denied you. Just as the real sun sustains life on this earth, that envisioned sun controls spiritual growth." Maybe it was God; maybe it was the broccoli spears. It was *something*. Walter Kowalski soon grew into the picture of the star athlete in his mind.

In high school in Windsor during the late 1940s Walter Kowalski ran track and field and played football. Eventually, puzzling his parents and doctor, there was no trace of his heart murmur. He kept growing on the outside, and people noticed. His parents were not large, nor were his brother and sister. Walter realized he was different, which usually means that one is destined to tread alone in life. People told Walter he should think about playing semiprofessional football. But he went to college instead, to Assumption College in Windsor. It was during this period that he began to try to form in his mind a picture of the rest of his life. He stayed in college only a year — money was tight — and eventually took a job as an apprentice electrician at the Ford Motor plant in Detroit where his father worked.

For exercise Walter wrestled with some old high school chums down at the Y, routinely tossing opponents around the ring as if they were empty suitcases. "This guy asked me if I wanted to make ten bucks wrestling. I said I'd do it. Ten bucks was ten bucks. That was almost half of what I made a week at the Ford Plant."

Walter Kowalski lost his first professional wrestling match. He got creamed. He lost his second match, his third, his fourth. Some of the wrestlers, he noticed, wrestled "dirty"—they gouged eyes, twisted necks, kicked, bit, and tripped their oppponents. The crowd, he noticed, loved watching this sort of rough stuff.

A Detroit promoter invited him to go on the road with a show. Walter went to the Ford personnel office and asked for a few days off. He won his first match in St. Louis. In his mind he was finally somebody in the ring, but he really didn't have a name worth beans. He was wrestling guys with names like the Crusher, the Bruiser, and the Moondog Brothers. His manager suggested that, because Walter was tall and trim and his dark hair shown above a square, handsome face when it was slicked back, he should adopt a matinee idol name, so he became "Tarzan" Kowalski.

Meanwhile, he kept asking for time off from the plant to wrestle and was finally told, "The Ford Motor Company doesn't subsidize professional wrestling." He was canned. He became Tarzan Kowalski and hit the road full-time. He saved his money and bought out his contract from his manager for $600. He pictured a better life for himself. In 1951 he moved to St. Louis. His manager there asked him to change "Walter" to "Wladek" to give him a more ethnic appeal to certain fans. At that point he was still a good guy in the ring, and he was still getting his brains scrambled pretty well.

Walter began to question what he was doing in wrestling—his tactics. In America, people say good guys finish last. "I saw how these other guys were winning and getting large paydays while I was losing and getting banged up. I made up my mind that I would switch. I'd kick those guys around and see how they liked it. It was the smartest move I ever made."

In 1954 during a particularly wild match with Yukon Eric, Tarzan Kowalski climbed up on the ring post and hurled his 6-foot 7-inch, 275-pound body into the air above the ring. It was the kind of stunt that later became a standard crowd rouser with professional wrestlers—lots of balletic aerials and mat-blasting racket, more mental effect than physical devastation. In any case, that night who could blame Yukon Eric for being as startled by the move as the audience. He moved his head the wrong way, and Tarzan Kowalski landed on his cauliflower ear. The ear popped off, spouting blood. The crowd went crazy, and the sportswriters had a big time writing about the incident.

The next afternoon a contrite Kowalski went to see his victim in the hospital. "Yukon was sitting in bed with his head all bandaged up. He understood that it was an accident — that was the business. He looked absolutely ridiculous, this big lump of a man with his head all wrapped up. I took one look at him and started laughing." A reporter was present. Suddenly Tarzan Kowalski became Killer Kowalski.

From then on Killer Kowalski decided that if he was going to be a bad guy in the ring, he'd be the best bad guy there ever was. He pictured it in his mind. But there was still the spiritual questioner in him; he prayed to be good at being bad — not to maim but to sure as heck terrify his opponent and the audience. That year, 1954, he became a main eventer and wrestled all over America. He ruptured Tarzan Zorra's windpipe. He developed the "Killer stomp" and the "giant swing," a maneuver in which he hoisted his opponent up and wheeled him around in the air until he was senseless. Eventually he developed something called the "claw hold," whereby he buried his massive fingers in an opponent's solar plexus until the opponent submitted or passed out. The claw hold became Killer Kowalski's signature. Combined with his snarling ring personality, the hold transformed Killer Kowalski into a national figure. He gouged, punched, and twisted his way to celebrity. He appeared on the covers of magazines. He bought a large home in Montreal. All sorts of people came to him with business opportunities. Women sent him provocative letters, even marriage proposals.

For a while wrestling magazines attempted to write "revealing" stories on Killer Kowalski. They called him a mystery man, a paradox, a man with no past. They wondered why he had never married, why he traveled alone. They portrayed him as a lonely hulk going from airport to train depot, haunting movies and pinball arcades in search of diversion. They said he shunned the company of other wrestlers because he feared he was a freak; that he scorned his public. In a sense they were right.

Walter Kowalski was not a happy man. He knew there were no road maps to the kind of earthly dignity he was seeking, and he'd had his ups and downs. He was involved in a traffic accident that threatened to end his career; for a while he lost almost one hundred pounds and contemplated getting out of wrestling. A jewelry store he owned went bankrupt. But it was all part of the search, he believed. He quit reading about himself in the press. But he continued to read books — the Bible, the teachings of Buddha, metaphysics. A couple of years, while wrestling in Omaha, Nebraska, he'd picked up a book called *The "I Am" Discourses* of Saint Germain. He was deeply moved by what it said. In summary it held that by uttering the words and thinking of oneself in a perfect, positive nimbus of light, a follower of Saint Germain would find balm for his earthly travails; he would know the militant, earth-shattering power of love.

It sounded, he later reflected, so simple, but it threw Kowalski spiritually to the mat. "I went to my knees after reading that," he said. "Suddenly I realized what this power was that I had been looking for all along. This was the door I'd been searching for."

Walter Kowalski was never the same after that. The Killer fought his way back to glory. It was a good time for him. He was worse than ever in the ring. He became curious about the world; he bought an airplane and flew all over the country. He always traveled alone.

"I thought about getting married. I had girlfriends," he reflected. "But marriage just wasn't in the picture for me. To be great in wrestling you have to be able to pick up and go off someplace for a whole year. It's not an easy life. Not many women could have handled that."

In 1965 Kowalski sold his airplane and went to live in Australia for a year. He toured the Far East, Malaysia, and the Philippines. He went all over the planet taking pictures and fielding boos. The crowds loved to hate him, and he loved them for it. "When they shout all those terrible things at me," he speculated to a reporter, "it's a good thing because maybe they're getting something terrible out of themselves, like a poison. They won't go home and use it on someone who loves them. At least I understand it."

When he came home to America in 1967, he was probably at the apogee of what had been a blessedly strange career. The big show went on for almost a decade after that. In March 1977 Walter Kowalski hung up Killer Kowalski's tights after a match in Providence, Rhode Island. He believed it was time to teach what he had learned.

His school for professional wrestlers in Salem, Massachusetts, aroused all kinds of national attention. A television network sent a crew and had Killer Kowalski and his staff of teachers and students perform live on a late-night show. The school made its way onto television shows such as "Real People" and "Games People Play." David Letterman had the Killer flown down for a New York taping. Sometimes when Kowalski went on WBZ radio's "Larry Glick Show," the phones lit up for hours. Callers asked him for advice on almost any subject — fame, money, romance. The talk usually came to spiritual things, and they even asked about God. It was an unhappy world out there in the vast radio darkness. Walter Kowalski's message was not new. It was as old as the first candle lit to beat back the darkness.

The world according to Killer Kowalski was not a pleasant place. There was still much darkness; there was still much temptation. There was, he believed, satanic chaos loose in the human spirit — extant in rock groups that brazenly worshiped Satan and popular movies that celebrated not the universality of love but the allure of celestial wars. We're rearing a generation of babies who have nightmares about mushroom clouds — the tree with spreading roots.

When Walter Kowalski spoke of these things, as in coaching risky wrestling moves, he spoke quietly but urgently. "The past does not exist. If you believe it exists, you'll make the past your present. We become what we believe," he would say. "All that matters is what you make of this second. . . . If we desecrate the instant, we desecrate the future. We think about evil; we invite its presence. Life is momentum. . . . We must invite the beautiful things. We must create a picture of love in our minds and *concentrate* on it. If I do it, and you do it, and the next guy starts to do it, something begins to happen. It's the tree I spoke of . . . all those little axes."

It was now nearly noon under a hotly flaring sun, and the restaurant was empty. The two men took the elevator to the hotel lobby. Walter Kowalski wanted to find his way to a bookstore. Lately, he explained, he'd been thinking about building a house. He'd never built a house before, but if it was in a book, he could do it.

As Walter was crossing Government Plaza, a pair of businessmen in tan suits spied him and stopped talking. One of them opened his jacket and grabbed himself crazily at the rope of belly that hung over his belt. As he waggled himself absurdly, his necktie did a jig. "Hey, Killer!" he brayed loudly. "How about the claw hold!"

Walter Kowalski just smiled and walked on alone, heading for the bookstore across the street and the possibility of a better world. His feet were safely on the street and his eyes on a house filled with light.

SUSAN FEINBERG

Just Call Him "Dallas"

THE LAST THING Dallas Boushey ever expected was to be a distinguished professor. He grew up in South Burlington, Vermont, in the middle of the Depression and had to drop out of school after the eighth grade to scramble for odd jobs. Boushey's search for work led to a job at the animal research lab at the University of Vermont College of Medicine, sweeping floors and cleaning animal cages for $15 a week. He liked his job and was content to work as a janitor for the rest of his life.

Half a lifetime later, without ever taking a formal course or getting a college degree, Dallas Boushey was an authority on human anatomy and an assistant professor at the University of Vermont

College of Medicine. Undeterred by his limited education, he taught himself anatomy by reading complex medical books. After mastering a subject, he invented and designed dozens of unique, three-dimensional anatomical models that have been displayed at anatomy meetings in medical schools all over the country.

In 1972 Boushey, then called a "technician," became the first non-faculty member to receive the Teacher of the Year award from a graduating medical class. Six months later the university's board of trustees named him assistant professor of anatomy with tenure.

Boushey's cubbyhole office had no academic degrees decorating its walls. A worn Rembrandt print hung next to the Purina cat calendar pasted on his metal locker. A miniature skeleton dangled over this desk, where pictures of his infant grandson and his two dogs were prominently displayed. With pride he pointed out a picture of Camp Bakersfield, a cabin he built in the Vermont woods in 1967. But he was modestly silent about the silver plaques inscribed "Freshman's Friend" from the class of 1966; "Anatomist, Teacher and Friend" from the class of 1971; and "Teacher of the Year" from the class of 1972.

Rocking back and forth in his desk chair one day in 1983, Boushey reminisced, "My parents separated when I was very young, so I grew up with my grandparents. My grandfather worked freight for the railroad. I was forced out of high school because we couldn't afford to pay the tuition. We were poor but not poor enough to go on welfare."

Boushey liked working as a handyman at the animal research lab. "I took an interest in it, just like in everything I do," he said. He was punctual, never took time off, and put in extra hours cheerfully.

"Dallas's boss praised him highly," said Dr. Chester Newhall, who was then chairman of the anatomy department at the College of Medicine. "He described Dallas as a model employee who kept the place shining."

Three years later Newhall needed to recruit a technician to assist an anatomy professor. He remembered Boushey and offered him the job. "I was squeamish at first," Boushey admitted. "Handling cadavers was the last thing I thought I'd be able to do. I didn't even know what the word *anatomy* meant." Newhall assured him that if he didn't like his new job, he could always have his old one back.

Boushey was nervous walking into Dr. Walter Stultz's lab that first morning in 1940, but he plunged into his new duties, sweeping and mopping floors and assisting Stultz with embalming. He soon conquered his initial qualms about working with cadavers. After several weeks he mastered all of the embalming procedures and took over those responsibilities completely.

Startled by Boushey's ability, Stultz decided to teach him to assist with dissections. Together they developed a skeletal recovery program to retrieve bones for medical students to study. Their first project was dissecting the human arm. Fascinated by the work, Boushey felt frustrated by his lack of knowledge and began to ask questions.

"What were the names of the muscles and the bones? How were they attached? He wanted to know it all," Stultz said. "I taught him the information as we worked. He would remember the names and repeat them to me the next day. It was at this point that I realized Dallas was unique. Even with his lack of education, he had the innate intelligence to learn the material."

One evening Boushey borrowed a copy of *Gray's Anatomy* and took it home to study. "I wanted to understand better what I was doing," he explained. "I figured that the faster I learned, the better off I'd be." For a non-medical student, *Gray's Anatomy* was a labyrinth of complex jargon and diagrams. For a man with an eighth-grade education who hadn't read much except newspapers and magazines, it seemed almost incomprehensible.

But Boushey wasn't one to give up easily. Every night after dinner, armed with English and medical dictionaries, he wrestled patiently with the text. "When I make up my mind to do something, I do it," he said. "No one can ever learn all of it, but I tried to learn something new every day. When I saw words that I didn't understand, I'd look them up. My wife copied passages out of the book and quizzed me on the material." The next morning at work, Boushey discussed what he had learned with Stultz.

Dallas Boushey was slowly teaching himself anatomy. He drove himself to learn all the material that he could absorb — the esoteric as well as the fundamental. "Dallas would look up eponyms [uncommonly used names of parts of the body] in the dictionary," said Stultz, laughing. "He used to bandy these names about and try to mystify the faculty."

After two years of studying and performing dissections, Boushey had acquired a knowledge of anatomy that equaled or surpassed that of his colleagues. "Whenever *I* had a question," said

Dr. Newhall, "I would go to Dallas." Stultz decided that Boushey should start instructing students.

"I said to Dallas, 'You know enough now; go around to the students at the anatomy tables and answer their questions.'" Stultz recalled. Dallas protested, 'I can't do that; they'd stump me right away!' But one afternoon he reluctantly agreed to try. He walked into the lab at two. By five he was all smiles."

Despite his initial shyness, Boushey felt at ease with the students. "I knew what I was talking about; they didn't. I learned a lot from them: how to improve my vocabulary, which was terrible at the time, and how other people thought in contrast to the way that I was thinking. They talked about medicine in general, so I gleaned information from them."

"Students always called Dallas at home with their problems," said his wife, Mary. "He's so good-natured that he would tutor them for nothing. Often he'd stay over long hours at the lab helping them, while dinner got cold."

A former student observed, "Dallas was more on our level than the other professors were. He was gentle and down-to-earth. We could really talk to him." Another added, "He didn't have all that educational mush behind him. He could talk to us in simpler terms."

Medical students are often squeamish when they begin to work with cadavers. Sometimes a troubled student would drop into Boushey's office and chat — about anything but anatomy. Boushey would listen quietly. Sometimes he'd see a student slip into the anatomy lab after classes and spend time alone with the cadavers. "I try to let them know I'm sympathetic. But I stay out of their way and let them get used to the idea," he said.

During Boushey's first years of teaching, his classes frequently complained that the illustrations in their anatomy books were more confusing than enlightening. They were having trouble picturing the body in three dimensions. It occurred to Boushey one day that anatomy would be easier for his students to grasp if they had streamlined anatomical models that they could hold in their hands and examine. There were no such models at the College of Medicine. So Boushey turned inventor.

He collected stovepipe wires, coiled them to represent different parts of the nervous system, wrapped them in gauze, and painted them in latex. He completed his first model in 1944. In the following four decades he constructed models of almost every part of the human anatomy and displayed them at medical schools all over the country. In the sunny anatomy lab that housed his work, dozens of his models, painted yellow, red, and blue, glowed in glass cases, looking like delicate sculptures that fit easily in the palm of your hand. Boushey beamed when people would admire his craft and was quick to explain what each wire and each color on each model represented.

Back in the 1960s and early 1970s, administrators at the College of Medicine were scratching their heads over Boushey's official status. What to call this technician who had taught himself anatomy, was instructing students, and was inventing anatomical models? "They didn't know what to do with me," Boushey recalled with a grin. "They kept giving me titles: senior technician, then demonstrator in anatomy."

In 1972 Dr. William Young, chairman of the anatomy department, recommended that the University of Vermont Board of Trustees designate Boushey a professor of anatomy. "When the graduating class gave him the Teacher of the Year award, that crystallized our thinking. The man had shown all of the skill and dedication of a superb teacher," Young said. The board agreed and approved his recommendation later that year.

Boushey refused to alter his lifestyle to accommodate his new rank. "Dallas is one of the most unchangeable people you can imagine," Mary Boushey said fondly. "He builds his models, teaches classes, and never stops reading anatomy. He feels uncomfortable at fancy parties. I've even seen him turn red when someone calls him professor. He's still the quiet, modest man that he was in 1937."

When asked the secret of his success, Boushey offered this advice: "Work hard. Just go along each day and take the bitter with the better. Do what you are told; like it or not, do it."

Nearly fifty years later, people at the University of Vermont College of Medicine seemed uniformly impressed with Boushey — except Boushey himself. "These days students ask me whether they should call me doctor or professor," he said, amused. "I tell them, 'Call me Dallas.' "